Seasonal
SALADS

Seasonal SALADS

150 versatile recipes

Reader's digest

CONTENTS

Salad basics
Salads for all seasons

Salads aren't just for summer – they can be warm, hearty and spicy, just as appetising in June as they are in January. By using seasonal ingredients, you will ensure maximum taste and nutrients all year round. Whatever the season, you can add flavour with some fresh herbs and ingredients such as garlic, chilli and ginger.

Inspiration for every season Look around the world for some inspiration – a spicy Asian noodle salad served chilled may be just the thing for a summer meal, but could do equally well served warm on a cold winter night. And an Italian-style salad of figs with prosciutto is perfect for a light summer or autumn lunch, as it makes the most of ripe figs. You can also take inspiration from the beautiful fresh produce that is available each season to create satisfying main meal salads and stunning side salads. When time is short, you can still prepare fabulous salads by combining fresh ingredients with high-quality ready-made products, such as pre-packaged salad mixes, canned beans and lentils.

Lettuces and other leafy greens Some lettuces have distinctive seasons, but many are available throughout the year, as they are frequently grown hydroponically. The main varieties are: crisphead or iceberg lettuces; butter-head lettuces; cos (romaine); and looseleaf lettuces.

Seasonal shopping Leafy greens and other fresh salad ingredients benefit from short transport distances from regional growers to local markets during their peak seasons. From a health perspective, this ensures that valuable nutrients are retained, but you will also appreciate the flavour of fresh, seasonal produce.

Seasonal fruits and vegetables Where possible, use produce that is grown locally in your own area as it will be the freshest and best. No seasonal guide can be definitive, as climate variations mean that produce may be available in, for example, late winter in one area, while it isn't ready until mid-spring in other regions. Also, there are many places where most produce is available cross-seasonally or throughout the entire year. Use the following list as a general guide to some of the fruits and vegetables that are best in each season.

Spring Artichokes, asparagus, grapefruit, green beans, peas, witlof (Belgian endive) and zucchini (courgettes).

Summer Berries and cherries, celery, chillies, cucumbers, figs, grapes, mangoes, nectarines, peaches, plums, radishes, tomatoes and watermelon.

Autumn Red and green apples, brussels sprouts, carrots, corn, fennel, grapes, mushrooms, parsnips, pears, plums, rhubarb and sweet potatoes (kumara).

Winter Red and green apples, beetroot (beet), cabbages, cauliflower, celeriac, kale, mandarins, olives, oranges, swede and turnips.

Ingredients available all year round Many fresh salad ingredients can be bought at any time of the year. Leafy greens, Asian greens, fresh herbs, rocket (arugula), onions, leeks, carrots, pumpkin, potatoes, sweet potatoes, mushrooms, cabbages, capsicums (bell peppers), radishes, cucumbers, fennel, tomatoes and zucchini (courgettes) are just some examples. The availability of a wide variety of lettuce, fruit and vegetables ensures you can prepare a range of fresh salads, whatever the season.

PREPARING SALADS

Trimming Remove outer, wilted and tough leaves from leafy greens and vegetables; remove any tough stalks, and pick over spinach and loose leaves.

Washing Wash leafy greens and spinach leaves in plenty of cold water. Wash herbs in bunches. If you are planning to use the zest of citrus fruits, buy untreated fruit if you can and scrub it under hot water. Wash well any vegetables that are not going to be peeled.

Spinning, drying and draining Use a salad spinner for large loose leaves, such as lettuce, baby spinach and rocket. Pat washed herbs dry between several layers of paper towel. Drain other fruit and vegetables well or dry with a clean tea towel.

Preparing Tear leaves into bite-sized pieces by hand; use a large cutting board and a large kitchen knife for all shredding or dicing jobs. Prepare salad dressings ahead if you wish. Most can be stored for 2–3 days if kept in the fridge in a clean, air-tight jar.

Secrets of a great salad

Brilliantly simple to toss together, salads offer endless scope for kitchen creativity. Side salads are a fantastic way to add seasonal colour and texture to your meal, while some salads are substantial enough to enjoy as a healthy meal on their own. Follow these ideas and tips for great salads, all year round.

Super salad combos Create the perfect balance of flavours and textures by combining seasonal fresh produce, protein, grains or legumes, and perhaps a pantry staple or two, tossed through with a dressing of your choice. Here are a few ideas:

✻ Vegetables – choose the freshest seasonal produce, in an array of colours, textures and flavours.

✻ Protein – add some cooked poultry, meat or seafood, such as tuna, salmon or prawns (shrimp).

✻ Grains and legumes – add some cooked pasta, noodles, rice, couscous, chickpeas, lentils, tofu, corn or canned beans.

✻ For extra flavour and texture – toss in some capers, olives, croutons, toasted nuts or seeds, fried bacon, prosciutto or pancetta, or crumbled fetta, blue cheese or grated parmesan.

Tips for a great salad

✻ Salads are usually best made just before serving, although most dressings can be made a day ahead.

✻ Before adding them to a salad, blanch any hard vegetables (such as broccoli) first, then briefly plunge into cold water to retain their colour and to quickly stop them cooking.

✻ For added flavour and sweetness, toss in some fruit, such as cranberries, blueberries, strawberries, apple slices or grapes.

✻ Instead of a dressing, simply drizzle a salad with a flavoured oil, such as hazelnut, walnut or avocado.

✻ A salad that contains a variety of fruits and vegetables may not need any dressing at all – just a fresh squeeze of lemon, lime or orange juice.

HANDY INGREDIENTS TO KEEP IN STOCK

From the pantry dried herbs and spices, instant rice, noodles, pasta, couscous, burghul (bulgur), vinegars and oils, honey, liquid seasonings (e.g. soy sauce), various nuts and seeds.

Preserves and long-life products olives, artichoke hearts, corn kernels, chargrilled capsicum (bell pepper), pickled cucumbers and gherkins, chutneys, tuna, beans, evaporated milk. Specialty oils and vinegars.

From the fridge bacon, cream, crème fraîche, yogurt, cottage cheese, opened jars of mayonnaise, tomato sauce (ketchup), mustard, ready-made salad dressings, grated horseradish, capers and sun-dried tomatoes in oil.

From the freezer vegetables and herbs.

Utensils for quick and easy salads There is an array of large and small utensils that can help make your life easier and save you time in the kitchen.

✽ A food processor with various attachments for slicing, grating and shredding is useful if you often find yourself preparing substantial quantities of vegetables or cheese.

✽ A vegetable grater or multi-function grater should be of good quality and work reliably. Micro-graters are available in different sizes for different vegetables. They make any grating or shredding job easy, and are particularly useful for quickly grating small amounts of citrus zest or parmesan.

✽ A shaker allows you to mix salad dressings quickly and simply; alternatively just use a small screw-top jar. Left-over dressing can be stored in the jar or shaker in the fridge.

✽ A standard-size whisk is essential to prepare dressings directly in the salad bowl. Use a small, cup-size whisk to prepare dressings in a cup or small bowl.

✽ A salad spinner comprises a bowl, a strainer insert and a lid. Salad spinners are useful for washing, drying and storing lettuce leaves.

✽ Use an apple corer to remove the cores before grating or slicing whole, washed apples.

A riot of salad leaves

A salad can comprise a medley of different leaves, with varying colours, flavours and textures. There is an ever-increasing selection of salad leaves available, ranging from delicate pale green leaves to vivid red leaves with a robust flavour and crisp texture.

CHOOSING LEAVES

A leafy salad needs a good mix of colours, flavours and textures. Salad leaves contain such a high proportion of water that you need to use a large quantity in order to supply a reasonable amount of valuable nutrients.

Sweet and mild

The light, subtle flavour of soft, sweet salad leaves makes them an excellent base for a simple side salad with a vinaigrette, or for salads made with other delicately flavoured ingredients.

Beetroot (beet) leaves These are dark green or reddish-green with a red stalk. Use young leaves as older ones may be tough.

Butter (Boston) lettuce This has soft mid-green outer leaves and a slightly crisper, paler heart.

Cos (romaine) lettuce This has a long, oval head of tightly packed crisp leaves.

English spinach Dark green English spinach leaves have a slightly metallic flavour due to their high iron content. Use baby leaves raw in salads.

Iceberg lettuce This pale, ball-shaped, tightly packed lettuce has crisp leaves with a refreshing but bland flavour.

Lamb's lettuce (mâche) These small rosettes of mid-green leaves have a velvety texture and delicate flavour.

Little gem lettuce This smaller variety of cos has crisp green outer leaves and delicate yellow inner leaves, with a sweet flavour.

Oakleaf lettuce This loose-leaf lettuce has soft, tender leaves and a pleasant mild flavour.

Red chard This has red stalks and mid- to deep-green leaves sometimes tinged with red. Use young leaves in salads.

Red coral lettuce This loose-leaf lettuce has leaves tinged deep red, with a tender, crisp texture and a bland flavour.

HERBS FOR SALADS

Fresh herbs can give a wonderful burst of flavour to a salad.
- Basil's small leaves have a pungent and fresh flavour.
- Snip chives over meat, poultry, fish or leaf salads.
- Powerful, spicy-tasting coriander (cilantro) leaves are an essential ingredient in Asian and Mexican-style salads.
- The mild caraway taste of feathery dill leaves works well in seafood, potato and cucumber salads.
- Mint is perfect in potato and bean salads as well as with fruit such as melon and mango.
- Use oregano or marjoram in tomato salads or warm salads with eggplant (aubergine) or lamb.

Bitter and strong

In general, darker salad leaves have a stronger flavour than pale ones, and just a few sprigs of a peppery green such as rocket (arugula) or watercress will provide delightful contrast in a salad of sweet leaves.

Chicory (curly endive) The large, round, slightly flattened heads have finely divided, mid-green leaves with a bitter flavour.

Green coral lettuce This loose-leaf lettuce has a mild flavour (but stronger than red coral).

Mizuna This deeply divided, pretty green leaf has a strong and peppery flavour.

Mustard cress This is a mixture of seedlings of garden cress and white mustard, used as a garnish.

Nasturtium leaves These attractive leaves have a peppery flavour and succulent texture.

Radicchio rosso This has crisp, deep red and white leaves with a slightly bitter, nutty flavour.

Rocket (arugula) This leaf has deep green, elongated frilled leaves with a pungent flavour.

Sorrel These leaves are mid-green and oval or spear shaped, with a lemony, refreshing flavour.

Watercress This has small, dark green leaves and tender stalks.

Witlof (Belgian endive) This has small, spear-shaped heads of pale leaves tinged with yellow or red at the tips.

mixed salad leaves

nasturtium

oakleaf lettuce

rocket

radicchio rosso

cos lettuce

baby beetroot leaves

Classic salad dressings

Vinaigrettes and other dressings are the essential link between the individual salad ingredients, bringing them all together to make a wonderful blend of flavours, colours and textures.

VINAIGRETTES

A classic vinaigrette is prepared with vinegar and oil, although lemon juice can be substituted for the vinegar. Generally use one part vinegar for three parts oil, but the ideal ratio will depend on the acidity of the vinegar or lemon juice used.

A classic vinaigrette can be whipped up just before serving, then drizzled over fresh green salad leaves. The ingredients are pantry staples, so it's a quick and easy gourmet touch that's not costly.

BASIC INGREDIENTS

Salad dressings generally contain an acidic element, an oil and any number of flavourings.

Vinegars

The classic is red or white wine vinegar (red has a slightly more robust flavour). Sherry vinegar has an even fuller flavour, but richest of all is balsamic vinegar. It is often sprinkled over a salad on its own as a dressing. Apple cider vinegar is good with salads that contain cheese. Rice vinegar, with its delicate flavour, is traditional in Asian dressings. **Vinegar substitutes** Substitutes for vinegar include lemon, lime, orange or grapefruit juice, or verjuice, which is the sour juice of unripe grapes.

Oils

Extra virgin cold-pressed oils are the 'top of the range' when it comes to oils. They are produced with minimal heat and refining processes. Blended vegetable oils that have been highly refined (the paler the colour, the more refined they are) have little goodness left in them. Choosing the right oil is vital to the success of your dressing. Olive oil is the classic for most vinaigrettes. Olive oil is like wine – different varieties of olive will give the oil its own special properties, and it can be peppery, salty, creamy, fruity or mild. Have at least one basic mild extra virgin olive oil and then experiment with others. Sunflower and peanut (groundnut) oils are good for lighter salad dressings. Walnut and hazelnut oils work well with chicken or spinach salads, and can be mixed with olive oil or another oil. Sesame oil, good in Asian salad dressings, has a smoky, nutty flavour.

Flavourings

Add a pinch of salt or a dash of soy or fish sauce; sweeten the dressing with a little sugar or honey; add spices such as ginger, garlic, chilli, mustard or wasabi; and add fresh or dried herbs such as thyme, lemon thyme, sage, tarragon, lemon myrtle, lemongrass and makrut (kaffir lime) leaves.

A QUICK HOMEMADE FRENCH DRESSING

Put **⅓ cup (80 ml) extra virgin olive oil, 1 tablespoon wine vinegar, a pinch of sugar or ½ teaspoon honey, ½ teaspoon dijon or wholegrain mustard** and **a pinch of salt and freshly ground black pepper** into a screw-top jar, then firmly seal and shake well. (Make double the quantity to save time.) Store the dressing in the fridge for up to 1 week. Because the oil may solidify, allow the dressing to return to room temperature about 30–60 minutes before use. Shake well before using. Serves 4.

Substitutes For the vinegar, use lemon or orange juice, or add a dash of balsamic vinegar. For extra flavour, add any of the following: 1 crushed clove garlic; 1 tablespoon freshly chopped herbs; 1 finely chopped red chilli; or a dash of hot chilli sauce.

SUPER CLASSIC SALAD DRESSINGS

Classic vinaigrette
Mix 2 tablespoons balsamic vinegar or lemon juice with ¼ cup (60 ml) extra virgin olive oil. Season with salt and black pepper. Add ½ teaspoon caster (superfine) sugar and some chopped fresh or dried herbs, if desired.

French dressing
Combine 1 tablespoon red wine vinegar and ¼ cup (60 ml) extra virgin olive oil with 1 teaspoon each of dijon mustard, salt and caster (superfine) sugar.

Mustard dressing
Combine 2 tablespoons olive oil, 2 tablespoons white wine vinegar and 1 tablespoon wholegrain mustard, and season with salt and black pepper.

Asian dressing
Mix 2 tablespoons lemon juice with 2 tablespoons soy sauce, 2 teaspoons sesame oil and 2 teaspoons finely grated fresh ginger. Stir in 1 teaspoon fish sauce, if desired.

Oil-free dressing
Combine 2 tablespoons rice vinegar with 1 tablespoon caster (superfine) sugar and ½ teaspoon salt.

German-style vinaigrette
Whisk 2 tablespoons white or red wine vinegar, a pinch of salt and black pepper until the salt has dissolved. Whisk in ⅓ cup (80 ml) olive oil, then flavour as desired with sugar, fruit juice, crushed garlic or mustard. Add a little stock to the vinaigrette to make it a little thinner and milder if you wish.

Creamy salad dressings

Mayonnaise is the classic base used for creamy dressings, but it is quite high in fat and kilojoules (calories). A healthier alternative can be made by mixing yogurt with mayonnaise. If using ready-made, choose a good-quality, egg-based one.

FLAVOURS FOR CREAMY DRESSINGS

Fresh herbs, finely chopped onions or spring onions (scallions), garlic and mustard make flavourful additions to both vinaigrettes and creamy dressings.

Creamy dressing ingredients The main ingredients for a creamy dressing are yogurt, cream, mayonnaise, crème fraîche or sour cream. But also try cottage cheese blended in a food processor to a creamy texture; it makes a rich dressing with minimal kilojoules and fat. Or try a blend of avocado, coriander (cilantro), yogurt, garlic and lime juice.

SUPER CREAMY SALAD DRESSINGS

Herb dressing Stir ²/₃ cup (160 g) natural (plain) yogurt and 75 g (2¹/₂ oz) crème fraîche together until combined. Stir in 3 teaspoons lemon juice and 1 teaspoon hot mustard, then add ¹/₂ teaspoon sugar, a large pinch of salt, or to taste, some freshly ground black pepper and 2 tablespoons chopped mixed fresh herbs (such as parsley, dill, chives). Stir in 1–2 tablespoons milk to thin the dressing, if desired.

Hummus dressing Dilute hummus with water, lemon juice or orange juice until it reaches the preferred consistency.

Roquefort dressing Finely mash 50 g (1³/₄ oz) roquefort cheese with a fork in a bowl. Add ¹/₂ cup (125 g) crème fraîche or light sour cream and stir to combine.

Homemade mayonnaise

Homemade mayonnaise is far better than anything out of a jar. It's easy to make, and you can add your own flavours. A light olive oil is best as extra virgin oil gives a strong flavour.

2 egg yolks
1 teaspoon dijon mustard
1 tablespoon lemon juice
300 ml (10 fl oz) light olive oil
salt
ground white pepper

Process the egg yolks, dijon mustard and lemon juice in a food processor for 1 minute, until combined and creamy. With the motor running, add the oil, a few drops at a time at first. As the mixture starts to thicken, add the oil in a thin stream – when all the oil has been added the mayonnaise should be thick and creamy. Season with salt and white pepper. Store the mayonnaise in an airtight container in the fridge for up to 1 week. Thin with lemon juice if needed.

Makes 1¹/₃ cups (340 g)

WAYS WITH MAYONNAISE

There are endless ways to jazz up mayonnaise, whether you're making it from scratch, or using a good-quality version from a jar. Add the following ingredients to 1 cup (250 g) mayonnaise. If you prefer, you can use ¹/₂ cup (125 g) mayonnaise mixed with ¹/₂ cup (125 g) natural (plain) yogurt, sour cream or crème fraîche.

Aïoli 2 crushed garlic cloves
Curry 1 tablespoon curry powder
Herb ¹/₂ cup (about 30 g) chopped mixed fresh herbs, such as chives, parsley, basil and thyme
Horseradish 2 tablespoons grated horseradish from a jar and 2 tablespoons finely snipped fresh chives
Lime or lemon 2 teaspoons grated zest and 1 tablespoon juice
Mustard 1 tablespoon dijon mustard
Wasabi 2 teaspoons lime or lemon juice and 1–2 teaspoons wasabi (Japanese horseradish).

Spring

Spring is the perfect time to prepare light, fresh salads bursting with the new season's crisp and tender vegetables – asparagus, cucumber, beans, radishes and various kinds of peas, are all at their best in spring.

Cucumber and pear salad

Good edible flowers to use in this salad include borage, violets, chive flowers, calendula, roses and nasturtiums. Always make sure you are using unsprayed flowers – if not grown yourself, then purchased from a greengrocer rather than a florist.

PREPARATION 15 minutes
SERVES 6

2 Lebanese or other small cucumbers

2 nashi or other yellow-skinned pears

75 g (2½ oz) soft goat's cheese, crumbled

2 tablespoons fresh dill sprigs

edible flowers, to garnish

freshly ground black pepper

Dressing

1½ tablespoons extra virgin olive oil

3 teaspoons white balsamic vinegar

salt

1 Use a mandolin or vegetable peeler to cut the cucumbers lengthwise into thin ribbons. Cut the pears lengthwise into quarters, discarding the cores, and thinly slice. Arrange the cucumber ribbons and pear slices on a large serving platter or in a shallow bowl.

2 Scatter the goat's cheese over the cucumbers and pears, and sprinkle with the dill.

3 To make the dressing, whisk the oil and vinegar in a small bowl until well combined. Season with salt.

4 Drizzle the dressing over the salad and scatter the flowers over the top. Season with freshly ground black pepper, and serve immediately.

If you can't find white balsamic vinegar, you could use verjuice, which is made from the juice of unfermented grapes and has a slight sweetness, too. White wine vinegar with a few drops of honey or raspberry vinegar would also be good.

Per serving
503 kJ, 120 kcal, 3 g protein, 8 g fat
(3 g saturated fat), 8 g carbohydrate
(8 g sugars), 2 g fibre, 177 mg sodium

Spinach salad with goat's cheese

Serve this simple salad with fresh, crusty sourdough bread for a quick, light lunch or supper. Crumbled fetta would also work well instead of the sliced goat's cheese.

PREPARATION 15 minutes
SERVES 4

250 g (8 oz) red cherry tomatoes

4½ cups (200 g) baby spinach leaves

160 g (5½ oz) goat's cheese, sliced into 8 rounds

20 fresh basil leaves

balsamic vinegar, to serve

Balsamic vinaigrette

1 tablespoon white balsamic vinegar

1½ teaspoons raspberry vinegar

freshly ground black pepper

¼ cup (60 ml) olive oil

1 Halve or quarter the tomatoes, depending on their size.

2 To make the vinaigrette, mix the balsamic vinegar with the raspberry vinegar and a little freshly ground black pepper. Whisk in the olive oil.

3 Put the spinach leaves in a large bowl. Add the vinaigrette and toss to coat the spinach leaves. Add the tomatoes and gently toss together.

4 Divide the salad among four serving plates. Arrange two rounds of goat's cheese and five basil leaves on top of each salad. Drizzle the goat's cheese with balsamic vinegar and serve immediately.

Briefly toast some slivered almonds or pine nuts and sprinkle them over the salad as a crunchy topping.

Per serving
1218 kJ, 291 kcal, 10 g protein, 26 g fat (10 g saturated fat), 5 g carbohydrate (4 g sugars), 2 g fibre, 232 mg sodium

Asian rice salad

Fragrant Thai jasmine rice works well for this Asian-style salad. Add some sliced, cooked chicken for a more substantial salad. If you like it spicy, add a little chopped fresh chilli or dried red chilli flakes to the dressing.

PREPARATION 10 minutes
COOKING 15 minutes
SERVES 2

⅔ cup (135 g) long-grain white rice

4 baby corn, diagonally sliced

8 snow peas (mangetout), thinly sliced

½ small red capsicum (bell pepper), chopped

2 stalks celery, thinly sliced

2 spring onions (scallions), thinly sliced

2 tablespoons raw cashew nuts

Ginger dressing

1 tablespoon vegetable oil

1 tablespoon salt-reduced soy sauce

1 tablespoon rice vinegar

½ teaspoon grated fresh ginger

1 Add the rice to a saucepan of boiling water and cook for 10–12 minutes, until just tender, adding the corn for the last 2 minutes of cooking. Drain and rinse the rice and corn under cold running water.

2 Transfer the rice and corn to a salad bowl along with the snow peas, capsicum, celery and spring onions, and toss until well combined.

3 To make the dressing, whisk together the oil, soy sauce, rice vinegar and ginger in a small bowl.

4 Pour the dressing over the salad and toss to evenly coat the rice and vegetables. Sprinkle with the cashew nuts and serve immediately.

If you prefer toasted cashew nuts, spread the nuts on a baking tray and roast in a 180°C (350°F/Gas 4) oven for about 5 minutes, until golden. Watch the nuts as they burn easily.

Per serving
1665 kJ, 398 kcal, 8 g protein, 13 g fat (2 g saturated fat), 59 g carbohydrate (3 g sugars), 3 g fibre, 400 mg sodium

Chargrilled asparagus and capsicum salad

Here, spears of asparagus, spring onions and capsicums are cooked
in a chargrill pan, then mixed with oven-baked parmesan croutons.
If you don't have a chargrill pan, the vegetables can be cooked on
a barbecue instead.

PREPARATION 30 minutes
COOKING 10 minutes
SERVES 4

500 g (1 lb) asparagus spears, trimmed

2 large red capsicums (bell peppers),
   halved lengthwise

250 g (8 oz) spring onions (scallions),
   trimmed

2 tablespoons extra virgin olive oil

parmesan shavings, to serve

Parmesan croutons

2 thick slices white bread, crusts
   removed, diced

1 tablespoon extra virgin olive oil

salt

freshly ground black pepper

⅓ cup (35 g) grated parmesan

Lemon and basil dressing

2 tablespoons lemon juice

2 tablespoons extra virgin olive oil

16 fresh basil leaves, torn into pieces

1 clove garlic, very finely chopped

salt

freshly ground black pepper

1 Preheat the oven to 180°C (350°F/Gas 4). Heat a chargrill
pan. Put the asparagus, capsicums and spring onions in
a bowl, add the oil and toss to coat.

2 Arrange the asparagus and capsicums in the hot chargrill
pan in a single layer. Cook the vegetables for 10 minutes,
until tender, adding the spring onions after the asparagus
and capsicums have been cooking for a few minutes. Turn
the vegetables frequently so they cook and colour evenly.
(You may have to cook the vegetables in two batches,
depending on the size of the pan.)

3 Meanwhile, to make the croutons, put the bread cubes in
a bowl with the oil, season with salt and freshly ground
black pepper, and toss well. Spread on a baking tray and
bake for 5 minutes. Sprinkle with the parmesan and bake
for a further 5 minutes, until golden and crisp.

4 To make the dressing, whisk the lemon juice, oil, basil and
garlic in a salad bowl, and season with salt and freshly
ground black pepper.

5 Roughly slice the chargrilled vegetables, add to the salad
bowl and stir to coat with the dressing. Scatter the croutons
over the top and garnish with a few shavings of parmesan.
Serve while still warm.

Per serving
*1430 kJ, 342 kcal, 10 g protein, 27 g fat
(5 g saturated fat), 16 g carbohydrate
(7 g sugars), 5 g fibre, 542 mg sodium*

Sardine salad with almonds

High in omega-3 fatty acids from the sardines, this salad is also rich in anti-oxidants, thanks to the orange, almonds and salad leaves. You could use fresh sardine fillets for this recipe.

PREPARATION 15 minutes
COOKING 10 minutes
SERVES 2

½ small red onion, thinly sliced

4 cups (180 g) mixed salad leaves, baby spinach leaves or rocket (arugula)

1 red capsicum (bell pepper), cut into flat pieces

1 yellow capsicum (bell pepper), cut into flat pieces

2 x 110 g (3½ oz) cans sardines in springwater, drained

¼ cup (40 g) raw almonds, sliced

Orange dressing
juice and grated zest of 1 orange

freshly ground black pepper

2 tablespoons extra virgin olive oil

1 Preheat a grill (broiler) or chargrill pan to high.

2 To make the dressing, whisk the orange juice and zest with some freshly ground black pepper in a salad bowl. Continue whisking while gradually adding the oil.

3 Add the onion and salad leaves to the salad bowl and toss to coat with the dressing.

4 Put the capsicums on the grill rack or in the chargrill pan and cook, turning several times, for 8–10 minutes, until the skin is charred and the flesh is tender. Set aside to cool.

5 While the capsicums are cooling, use a small sharp knife to split the sardines lengthwise and remove the backbones.

6 Peel off the capsicum skin and cut the flesh into strips. Stir the capsicums and sardines into the salad. Sprinkle the almonds over the top and serve.

 If you are using fresh sardines, grill (broil) or chargrill 3–4 fillets per person after you cook the capsicums. Cook the sardines for 2 minutes without turning.

Per serving
1993 kJ, 476 kcal, 24 g protein, 37 g fat (5 g saturated fat), 12 g carbohydrate (12 g sugars), 5 g fibre, 111 mg sodium

Chicken, avocado and brie salad

PREPARATION 10 minutes
SERVES 4

2 smoked chicken breasts, about 150 g (5 oz) each
125 g (4 oz) brie
125 g (4 oz) mixed salad leaves
1 avocado
¼ cup (60 ml) sushi vinegar

1 Discard the skin from the chicken breasts. Shred or roughly chop the flesh and place it in a salad bowl.

2 Slice the brie, then add it to the salad bowl along with the salad leaves.

3 Cut the avocado in half and remove the stone. Thickly slice the flesh and add it to the salad bowl.

4 Drizzle the sushi vinegar over the salad and gently toss together. Serve immediately, with some crusty bread for lunch or brunch.

Substitute fetta or blue cheese for the brie in this recipe. Add some sliced pear or mango when in season. Use barbecued chicken or smoked turkey.

Per serving
1698 kJ, 406 kcal, 25 g protein, 32 g fat
(11 g saturated fat), 2 g carbohydrate
(2 g sugars), 1 g fibre, 254 mg sodium

Mixed bean salad

PREPARATION 10 minutes
COOKING 5 minutes
SERVES 4

250 g (8 oz) green beans, trimmed
420 g (15 oz) can mixed beans, rinsed and drained
250 g (8 oz) red cherry tomatoes, halved
1¾ cups (60 g) baby rocket (arugula)
2 tablespoons Italian dressing

1 Steam, microwave or boil the green beans for 2–3 minutes, until just softened. Drain and refresh under cold running water, then drain again and place in a large salad bowl.

2 Add the mixed beans, tomatoes and rocket to the salad bowl with the green beans.

3 Just before serving, drizzle the Italian dressing over the salad and toss together.

Add black olives and diced haloumi or sliced bocconcini (fresh baby mozzarella balls). Add blanched broad (fava) beans, or thinly sliced raw green or yellow zucchini (courgette).

Per serving
458 kJ, 110 kcal, 6 g protein, 4 g fat (<1 g saturated fat), 13 g carbohydrate (4 g sugars), 7 g fibre, 336 mg sodium

Warm potato and broad bean salad

For a flavour-drenched warm salad, take nutty new potatoes and high-fibre broad beans, drizzle them with a herb vinaigrette, then serve on beetroot leaves or mixed salad leaves.

PREPARATION 20 minutes
COOKING 15 minutes
SERVES 4

500 g (1 lb) baby new potatoes

1 kg (2 lb) fresh broad (fava) beans or 300 g (10 oz) frozen shelled baby broad (fava) beans

100 g (3½ oz) beetroot (beet) leaves or mixed salad leaves

⅓ cup (20 g) snipped fresh chives

Herb vinaigrette

1 teaspoon sugar

1 teaspoon English mustard

1 teaspoon cider vinegar

¼ cup (60 ml) olive oil

3 large sprigs fresh thyme

salt

freshly ground black pepper

1 Add the potatoes to a large saucepan of boiling water. Bring back to a boil, then reduce the heat, cover and cook for 10 minutes.

2 Meanwhile, shell the broad beans, if you are using fresh ones. Soak the shelled beans in hot water for 3–4 minutes before peeling off the pale green outer skins. Add the beans to the potatoes, then bring back to a boil, cover and cook for 4 minutes, until tender. Drain well.

3 To make the vinaigrette, whisk the sugar, mustard and vinegar in a large bowl until the sugar has dissolved. Whisk in the oil and rub the thyme leaves off the stalks and into the bowl. Season with salt and freshly ground black pepper.

4 Make a bed of beetroot or salad leaves on four plates. Stir the potatoes and beans into the vinaigrette. Sprinkle with the chives and mix again. Top the leaves with the potato and bean salad.

Choose small, young beetroot leaves, or if only older ones are available, reduce their quantity by half and combine them with sweeter leaves, such as lamb's lettuce (mâche), oakleaf lettuce, or some finely shredded Chinese cabbage.

Per serving
1099 kJ, 263 kcal, 10 g protein, 18 g fat (2 g saturated fat), 21 g carbohydrate (3 g sugars), 9 g fibre, 176 mg sodium

Green bean and bacon salad

Add a large can of drained, flaked tuna and some red cherry tomatoes to this salad, and serve with some crusty bread for a light main meal.

PREPARATION 10 minutes
COOKING 10 minutes
SERVES 6

1 cup (155 g) frozen broad (fava) beans
500 g (1 lb) baby green beans, trimmed
5 slices bacon, rind removed

Dressing
¼ cup (60 ml) red wine vinegar
⅓ cup (80 ml) extra virgin olive oil
1 teaspoon dijon mustard
pinch of soft brown sugar
¼ teaspoon salt
freshly ground black pepper

1 Cook the broad beans in a saucepan of boiling water for 5 minutes, until just tender. Drain and rinse under cold water until cool, then peel off the pale green outer skins.

2 Meanwhile, cook the green beans in a saucepan of boiling water for 1–2 minutes, until just tender. Drain and rinse under cold water until cool.

3 Cook the bacon in a small frying pan over medium heat until crisp. Drain on paper towel.

4 To make the dressing, combine the vinegar, oil, mustard, sugar, salt and some freshly ground black pepper in a small screw-top jar. Shake well to combine.

5 Put the green beans and broad beans in a wide serving bowl and pour the dressing over the top. Roughly chop the bacon, pile it on the salad and serve immediately.

Per serving
806 kJ, 193 kcal, 10 g protein, 16 g fat
(3 g saturated fat), 3 g carbohydrate
(1 g sugars), 3 g fibre, 654 mg sodium

Couscous and chickpea salad

This quick and easy salad goes especially well with chargrilled or barbecued chicken or fish, pan-fried lamb cutlets, or seared lamb backstraps or loin fillets.

PREPARATION 10 minutes
COOKING 10 minutes
SERVES 2

½ cup (95 g) instant couscous

2 tablespoons currants

2 tablespoons slivered almonds

2 tablespoons olive oil

½ red onion, finely chopped

½ red capsicum (bell pepper), finely chopped

1 teaspoon ground cumin

½ cup (60 g) canned chickpeas

6 pitted green olives, quartered

1½ tablespoons chopped fresh parsley

1 tablespoon lemon juice

salt

freshly ground black pepper

1 Put the couscous and currants in a heatproof bowl. Add ½ cup (125 ml) boiling water. Cover with foil and stand for 5 minutes, until all the water has been absorbed. Fluff the couscous with a fork to break up any lumps.

2 Meanwhile, toast the almonds in a dry non-stick frying pan over medium heat, stirring occasionally, for 3–4 minutes, until lightly golden. Remove from the pan.

3 Heat 2 teaspoons of the oil in the pan over medium heat. Cook the onion and capsicum, stirring, for 3–4 minutes, until softened.

4 Add the cumin, chickpeas, olives, almonds, parsley, lemon juice and remaining oil to the pan. Stir in the couscous and season with salt and freshly ground black pepper. Serve immediately, or cover and refrigerate until required.

Use any left-over chickpeas to make hummus. Blend them with crushed garlic, olive oil, tahini, ground cumin and lemon juice. Serve as a dip or sandwich spread.

Per serving
1765 kJ, 422 kcal, 10 g protein, 23 g fat (3 g saturated fat), 44 g carbohydrate (3 g sugars), 4 g fibre, 79 mg sodium

Five-spiced duck and noodle salad

Instead of cooking the duck breasts, buy a Chinese barbecued duck, shred the meat and toss it through the salad. You may not need to use quite as much soy sauce to dress the salad.

PREPARATION 10 minutes

COOKING 15 minutes

SERVES 4

1 teaspoon Chinese five-spice

2½ tablespoons salt-reduced soy sauce

4 boneless duck breasts with skin

450 g (15 oz) thin hokkien (egg) noodles

1 tablespoon peanut (groundnut) oil

100 g (3½ oz) Asian salad mix or mixed salad leaves

1 Combine the five-spice and 1 tablespoon of the soy sauce in a small bowl. Brush both sides of each duck breast with the mixture.

2 Heat a large non-stick frying pan over medium–high heat. Cook the duck breasts, skin side down, for 6 minutes, until golden brown and crisp. Turn and cook for 4 minutes for medium–rare, or until done to your liking. Transfer the duck to a plate and set aside for 5 minutes to rest.

3 Meanwhile, bring a saucepan of water to a boil. Add the noodles and cook for 2 minutes, until tender. Drain and rinse under cold running water, then drain again.

4 Using a large sharp knife, cut the duck across the grain into thin slices.

5 Whisk the remaining soy sauce with the peanut oil in a large bowl. Add the drained noodles and toss to coat. Add the salad leaves and duck slices, and gently toss to combine. Serve immediately.

You can replace the duck with chicken. For extra colour and crunch, toss some strips of capsicum (bell pepper) through the salad.

Per serving
3500 kJ, 836 kcal, 27 g protein, 67 g fat
(19 g saturated fat), 32 g carbohydrate
(2 g sugars), <1 g fibre, 624 mg sodium

Crunchy nut coleslaw

Made with cabbage, carrot and radishes, this colourful coleslaw is flecked with spring onions, sweet sultanas and roasted peanuts, and tossed with a creamy mayonnaise and yogurt dressing that is low in fat.

PREPARATION 15 minutes
SERVES 4

4 spring onions (scallions)

2⅔ cups (200 g) finely shredded cabbage

1 large carrot, coarsely grated

⅓ cup (40 g) sultanas (golden raisins)

30 g (1 oz) radishes, thinly sliced

⅓ cup (50 g) unsalted roasted peanuts (groundnuts)

¼ cup (15 g) chopped fresh parsley or snipped fresh chives, or a mixture of the two (optional)

Dressing

2 tablespoons mayonnaise

⅔ cup (160 g) low-fat natural (plain) yogurt

salt

freshly ground black pepper

1 Finely chop the spring onions, keeping the white and green parts separate.

2 Combine the cabbage, carrot, sultanas and white parts of the spring onions in a large bowl.

3 To make the dressing, stir the mayonnaise and yogurt together, and season with salt and freshly ground black pepper.

4 Stir the dressing into the cabbage mixture and toss to coat all the ingredients.

5 Just before serving, stir in the radishes and peanuts. Sprinkle with the green parts of the spring onions and the parsley or chives, if using.

Roasted peanuts are a nutritious addition to this recipe. Homemade coleslaw not only looks and tastes far superior to ready-made coleslaw, it is also much lower in fat.

Per serving
849 kJ, 203 kcal, 7 g protein, 13 g fat (2 g saturated fat), 15 g carbohydrate (14 g sugars), 4 g fibre, 136 mg sodium

Tomato, cucumber and artichoke salad

Spinach and herb wraps are toasted and broken into pieces to add some crunch to this salad. You could also use pita breads or tortillas, or simply sprinkle some ready-made croutons or crisp, broken gourmet crackers over the salad.

PREPARATION 10 minutes

COOKING 10 minutes

SERVES 4

2 spinach and herb wraps (flat breads)

cooking oil spray

125 g (4 oz) snow peas (mangetout)

250 g (8 oz) marinated artichokes in oil

2 Lebanese or other small cucumbers, finely chopped

250 g (8 oz) baby roma (plum) tomatoes, halved

1 Preheat the oven to 200°C (400°F/Gas 6). Lightly spray both sides of the spinach wraps with cooking oil. Place on a baking tray lined with baking (parchment) paper and bake for 8–10 minutes, until lightly browned. Set aside to cool, then break into bite-sized pieces.

2 Meanwhile, trim the snow peas and cut in half diagonally. Place in a heatproof bowl, cover with boiling water and soak for 1–2 minutes, until just softened. Drain and refresh under cold running water, then drain again and place on a large platter or in a large salad bowl.

3 Drain the artichokes, reserving the oil, and cut them into quarters. Add the artichokes, cucumbers and tomatoes to the salad.

4 Add the toasted wrap pieces to the salad and gently toss together. Drizzle with the reserved artichoke oil and serve immediately.

Try this salad with chargrilled chicken or steak. Replace the snow peas with blanched asparagus. Add watercress sprigs, julienned radishes or some thin strips of red capsicum (bell pepper).

Per serving
343 kJ, 82 kcal, 6 g protein, 1 g fat
(<1 g saturated fat), 11 g carbohydrate
(3 g sugars), 4 g fibre, 139 mg sodium

Potato and spring vegetable salad

PREPARATION 10 minutes
COOKING 10 minutes
SERVES 4

1 tablespoon (20 g) butter

1 tablespoon olive oil

½ small onion, finely chopped

2 cloves garlic, crushed

500 g (1 lb) baking (floury) potatoes, diced

12 asparagus spears, cut into short lengths

1 zucchini (courgette), diced

⅔ cup (100 g) fresh or frozen peas

2 tablespoons lemon juice

½ teaspoon dijon mustard

½ cup (10 g) fresh mint leaves, chopped

salt

freshly ground black pepper

grated parmesan, to serve (optional)

Make the most of spring's gorgeous green vegetables in this vibrant and healthy salad.

1 Heat the butter and oil in a small frying pan over medium heat. Add the onion and garlic, and sauté for 3 minutes, until softened.

2 Meanwhile, add the potatoes to a large saucepan of boiling water and cook for 3–4 minutes, until just tender. Add the asparagus, zucchini and peas. Cook for a further 1 minute, then drain well.

3 Tip the vegetables into a serving bowl, add the onion mixture, lemon juice, mustard and mint, and gently toss. Season well with salt and freshly ground black pepper. Serve warm, topped with grated parmesan, if using.

Per serving
794 kJ, 190 kcal, 6 g protein, 9 g fat,
(3 g saturated fat), 20 g carbohydrate
(3 g sugars), 5 g fibre, 208 mg sodium

Mixed leaf salad

PREPARATION 10 minutes
SERVES 6

150 g (5 oz) lettuce leaves

Dressing
2 tablespoons extra virgin olive oil
3 teaspoons white wine vinegar
½ teaspoon dijon mustard
salt
freshly ground black pepper

1 Place the lettuce in a large bowl of cold water and stand for
5 minutes. Working in batches of a handful at a time, lift the
leaves out and let the excess water drain away. Dry them
in a salad spinner and place in a salad bowl; repeat with
the remaining leaves. Cover tightly with plastic wrap and
refrigerate if not using immediately.

2 To make the dressing, combine the olive oil, vinegar and
mustard in a small screw-top jar. Shake well to combine,
then season with salt and freshly ground black pepper.

3 Just before serving, pour the dressing over the lettuce
and toss to coat the leaves. Don't add the dressing too
early, or the lettuce will become soggy.

This is the simplest of
all salads. Use one type
of lettuce, or a mixture.
Throw in some fresh
herbs, and experiment
with different vinegars
and oils in the dressing.

Per serving
*249 kJ, 60 kcal, <1 g protein, 6 g fat
(<1 g saturated fat), <1 g carbohydrate
(<1 g sugars), <1 g fibre, 115 mg sodium*

Cucumber, radish and snow pea salad

Snow peas and radishes are both great sources of folate and vitamin C, nutrients that work together to protect the health of your heart. Radishes were cultivated thousands of years ago in China, and they were so highly prized in ancient Greece that gold replicas were made of them.

PREPARATION 10 minutes

COOKING 5 minutes

SERVES 4

175 g (6 oz) snow peas (mangetout), trimmed

2 cucumbers, scored and thinly sliced

1 bunch (about 300 g/10 oz) radishes, thinly sliced

1 tablespoon toasted sesame seeds (optional)

Soy dressing

1 tablespoon rice vinegar

2 teaspoons sugar

2 teaspoons soy sauce

1 teaspoon dark sesame oil

pinch of salt

1 Cook the snow peas in a saucepan of boiling water for 2–3 minutes, until tender but still crisp. Drain and rinse under cold running water.

2 To make the dressing, whisk the rice vinegar, sugar, soy sauce, sesame oil and salt in a bowl until the sugar and salt have dissolved.

3 Combine the snow peas, cucumbers and radishes in a large salad bowl. Add the dressing and gently toss to combine. Sprinkle with the sesame seeds, if using, and serve immediately.

To toast the sesame seeds, cook them in a dry frying pan over medium heat for about 1 minute, stirring frequently, until they are lightly browned. Transfer to a plate to cool.

Per serving
242 kJ, 58 kcal, 3 g protein, 2 g fat (<1 g saturated fat), 8 g carbohydrate (7 g sugars), 2 g fibre, 283 mg sodium

Green bean, pea and mixed leaf salad

This beautiful salad is the essence of spring, a combination of crisp vegetables, prosciutto and goat's cheese topped with a balsamic dressing. Serve it with chicken or fish, with some boiled new potatoes tossed in butter.

PREPARATION 25 minutes
COOKING 10 minutes
SERVES 6–8

150 g (5 oz) snow peas (mangetout), trimmed

200 g (7 oz) green beans, trimmed

300 g (10 oz) fresh peas in the pod, shelled

1 cup (50 g) mixed salad leaves

4 slices prosciutto or pancetta, cut or torn into bite-sized pieces

3 radishes, thinly sliced

200 g (7 oz) goat's cheese, crumbled

salt

freshly ground black pepper

Dressing

2 tablespoons extra virgin olive oil

1 tablespoon balsamic vinegar

salt

freshly ground black pepper

1 Bring a saucepan of water to a boil, and prepare a bowl of iced water. Add the snow peas to the pan, return to a boil and cook for 1 minute. Lift out with a slotted spoon or tongs, allowing the water to drain off, then plunge into the iced water. Lift out and drain on paper towel.

2 Return the water to a boil and replenish the iced water. Add the beans to the pan, return to a boil and cook for 2 minutes. Lift out with a slotted spoon or tongs, then plunge into the iced water and drain on paper towel. Repeat with the peas, cooking them for 3 minutes and draining in a sieve before plunging into the iced water. The peas and beans should be bright green and tender but still crisp.

3 To make the dressing, whisk the olive oil and balsamic vinegar in a small bowl. Season with salt and freshly ground black pepper.

4 Arrange the snow peas, beans and peas with the salad leaves on a platter. Scatter the prosciutto or pancetta, radishes and goat's cheese over the top and drizzle with the dressing. Season with salt and freshly ground black pepper, and serve immediately.

For the best flavour, choose small or baby green beans if you can get them. If you buy fresh peas already shelled, you will need 1 cup (150 g). You could also use 1 cup (150 g) frozen peas, which only need to be cooked for 1 minute.

Per serving
807 kJ, 193 kcal, 11 g protein, 13 g fat (5 g saturated fat), 8 g carbohydrate (4 g sugars), 4 g fibre, 472 mg sodium

Smoked salmon and pea pasta salad

This colourful and nutritious salad is full of different textures and flavours. Little bows of pasta and tender peas are mixed with a creamy watercress and herb dressing, then topped with smoked salmon and garnished with watercress.

PREPARATION 20 minutes
COOKING 15 minutes
SERVES 4

250 g (8 oz) farfalle (pasta bows)

⅔ cup (100 g) fresh or frozen peas

100 g (3½ oz) watercress, trimmed

½ red onion, finely chopped

2 tablespoons capers, rinsed and squeezed dry

¼ telegraph (long) cucumber, diced

1 tablespoon sunflower or vegetable oil

1 tablespoon white wine vinegar, or to taste

125 g (4 oz) smoked salmon, cut into thin strips

Watercress and herb dressing

50 g (1¾ oz) watercress, trimmed

1 clove garlic

4 sprigs fresh parsley

2 sprigs fresh tarragon

5 spring onions (scallions), chopped

⅓ cup (90 g) low-fat natural (plain) yogurt

2 tablespoons mayonnaise

salt

freshly ground black pepper

1 Add the pasta to a large saucepan of boiling water and cook according to the packet instructions until al dente, adding the peas for the last 2–3 minutes. Drain the pasta and peas, rinse well with cold water, then drain again. Transfer to a large bowl.

2 While the pasta and peas are cooking, make the dressing. Finely chop the watercress in a food processor or blender. Add the peeled clove garlic, parsley, tarragon and half of the spring onions, and process to a fine purée. Add the yogurt and mayonnaise, and briefly process to combine. Stir in the remaining spring onions, and season with salt and freshly ground black pepper.

3 Add the dressing to the bowl with the pasta and peas, and mix well. Divide among four serving plates. Toss the watercress with the red onion, capers, cucumber, oil and vinegar, and spoon over the salad. Arrange the smoked salmon strips on top and serve.

Per serving
1550 kJ, 370 kcal, 19 g protein, 10 g fat (1 g saturated fat), 50 g carbohydrate (5 g sugars), 6 g fibre, 854 mg sodium

Chef's salad

One of the classic salads, chef's salad is quick and simple to prepare. Replace the mayonnaise dressing with a ready-made French dressing if you prefer. Serve the salad with grainy bread for a light lunch.

PREPARATION 10 minutes
COOKING 10 minutes
SERVES 2

2 eggs

100 g (3½ oz) baby cos (romaine) lettuce leaves

10 baby roma (plum) tomatoes, halved

1 small Lebanese or other small cucumber, chopped

2 slices ham off the bone, about 125 g (4 oz), cut into thick strips

2 slices jarlsberg cheese, cut into thick strips

freshly ground black pepper

Mayonnaise dressing

2 tablespoons mayonnaise

2 teaspoons lemon juice

1 teaspoon dijon mustard

1 teaspoon honey

salt

freshly ground black pepper

1 Put the eggs in a small saucepan, cover with cold water and bring to a boil over high heat. Reduce the heat and gently boil for 7 minutes, stirring occasionally. Drain the eggs and cool under cold running water. Leave to cool, then peel and cut into quarters.

2 Divide the lettuce leaves between two serving plates and arrange the tomatoes, cucumber, eggs, ham and cheese over the top.

3 To make the dressing, combine the mayonnaise, lemon juice, mustard and honey in a bowl. Season with salt and freshly ground black pepper, and mix until well blended.

4 Drizzle the dressing over the salad and serve immediately, sprinkled with freshly ground black pepper.

 Jarlsberg cheese is a mild, slightly sweet Swiss-style cheese. It's suitable for use on sandwiches, as a snack or in cooking. You can use any other Swiss-style cheese in this salad.

Per serving
1293 kJ, 309 kcal, 24 g protein, 19 g fat (6 g saturated fat), 11 g carbohydrate (10 g sugars), 3 g fibre, 1265 mg sodium

Fresh tuna and green bean salad

Succulent tuna mixed with crisp beans and olives makes a light and tasty salad. You can replace the tuna with pan-fried salmon, or omit the lettuce and toss the salad through cooked pasta.

PREPARATION 10 minutes
COOKING 10 minutes
SERVES 2

2 x 140 g (4½ oz) tuna steaks

salt

freshly ground black pepper

2 teaspoons olive oil

100 g (3½ oz) green beans, halved

12 yellow or red cherry tomatoes, halved

12 pitted kalamata olives

100 g (3½ oz) baby cos (romaine) lettuce leaves

Mustard vinaigrette

2 tablespoons olive oil

1 tablespoon red wine vinegar

1 teaspoon dijon mustard

pinch of caster (superfine) sugar

1 Season the tuna on both sides with salt and freshly ground black pepper. Heat the oil in a small non-stick frying pan over medium–high heat. Cook the tuna for 2–3 minutes on each side for medium–rare, or until cooked to your liking. Remove from the pan and set aside to cool. Slice or flake the tuna into chunks.

2 Meanwhile, bring a small saucepan of water to a boil. Add the beans and cook for 2 minutes, until just tender but still crisp. Drain and refresh under cold running water.

3 To make the vinaigrette, whisk the oil, vinegar, mustard and sugar in a large bowl.

4 Add the beans, tomatoes, olives and tuna to the bowl with the dressing and gently toss together. Arrange the lettuce leaves on two serving plates. Top with the tuna and bean mixture, and serve immediately.

Per serving
2281 kJ, 545 kcal, 38 g protein, 39 g fat (7 g saturated fat), 8 g carbohydrate (4 g sugars), 4 g fibre, 441 mg sodium

Mixed leaf salad with bocconcini and semi-dried tomatoes

This salad makes a perfect accompaniment to grilled meat or fish with Mediterranean flavours. Serve it with some fresh, crusty bread. You can save time by buying pre-packaged or loose mixed salad leaves.

PREPARATION 20 minutes
COOKING 1 minute
SERVES 4

½ frilly-edged lettuce, leaves separated

½ oakleaf lettuce, leaves separated

1 head young garlic

¼ cup (60 ml) olive oil

85 g (3 oz) semi-dried (sun-blushed) tomatoes in oil, drained and coarsely chopped

250 g (8 oz) bocconcini (fresh baby mozzarella balls), diced

1 tablespoon white balsamic vinegar

½ teaspoon dried oregano

freshly ground black pepper

1 Tear the lettuce leaves into bite-sized pieces and place in a large salad bowl.

2 Remove the outer, tough skin from the garlic head, then separate the individual cloves; they should come apart easily. Heat 1 tablespoon of the oil in a small non-stick frying pan over low heat. Gently cook the garlic cloves for 1 minute. Remove from the pan and set aside, reserving the oil in the pan for the dressing.

3 Toss the semi-dried tomatoes, bocconcini and garlic cloves with the lettuce leaves.

4 Mix the balsamic vinegar with the oregano and a little freshly ground black pepper. Whisk in the remaining olive oil and the reserved oil from the pan. Toss the dressing with the salad and serve immediately.

Young garlic is also known as spring garlic or green garlic. Its flavour is slightly less intense than regular garlic. There is no need to peel young garlic cloves. If young garlic is unavailable, use 2–3 spring onions (scallions) or French shallots instead.

Per serving
1287 kJ, 308 kcal, 13 g protein, 27 g fat (9 g saturated fat), 7 g carbohydrate (4 g sugars), 2 g fibre, 233 mg sodium

Burghul and quinoa salad

PREPARATION 15 minutes, plus 15 minutes cooling
COOKING 15 minutes
SERVES 4

75 g (2½ oz) burghul (bulgur)

75 g (2½ oz) quinoa

1 teaspoon sugar

grated zest and juice of 1 lemon

3 teaspoons olive oil

¼ cucumber, finely diced

2 large tomatoes, finely diced

1 large green capsicum (bell pepper), finely diced

2 spring onions (scallions), thinly sliced

5 large sprigs fresh mint, chopped

2 cups (60 g) chopped fresh flat-leaf parsley

freshly ground black pepper

1 cos (romaine) lettuce, to serve

Add fresh salad staples, plus aromatic parsley, mint and lemon to plump burghul grains for a zesty lunchtime treat that is refreshing and surprisingly filling.

1 Place the burghul and quinoa in a saucepan with 4 cups (1 litre) boiling water. Bring back to a boil, then reduce the heat, cover and simmer for 15 minutes, until tender. Drain in a sieve if any liquid remains.

2 Combine the sugar, lemon zest and lemon juice in a large bowl, stirring until the sugar dissolves. Whisk in the oil, then add the cucumber, tomatoes, capsicum and spring onions. Stir in the hot burghul and quinoa, then cover and leave to cool for 15 minutes.

3 Stir the mint and parsley into the salad and season with freshly ground black pepper.

4 Divide the salad among four bowls and serve with the lettuce leaves for wrapping and scooping.

Per serving
*800 kJ, 191 kcal, 7 g protein, 5 g fat
(2 g saturated fat), 28 g carbohydrate
(5 g sugars), 6 g fibre, 22 mg sodium*

Asparagus, avocado and snow pea salad

PREPARATION 15 minutes
COOKING 5 minutes
SERVES 4

200 g (7 oz) snow peas (mangetout), trimmed

500 g (1 lb) asparagus spears, cut into short lengths

2 ripe avocados, sliced crosswise

fresh chervil or parsley, to garnish

Raspberry vinaigrette

1 tablespoon raspberry vinegar

2 teaspoons balsamic vinegar

pinch of sugar (optional)

pinch of salt (optional)

freshly ground black pepper

⅓ cup (80 ml) sunflower or vegetable oil

1 Bring a large saucepan of water to a boil. Add the snow peas and cook for 2 minutes. Remove the snow peas with a slotted spoon and rinse with cold water. Drain well.

2 Add the asparagus to the boiling water and cook for 3 minutes. Pour into a large colander, rinse with cold water and drain well.

3 To make the vinaigrette, whisk the raspberry vinegar with the balsamic vinegar. Season with sugar, salt and freshly ground black pepper. Whisk in the oil.

4 Arrange the asparagus, snow peas and avocados on a serving plate. Drizzle with the vinaigrette and garnish with chervil or parsley.

We have used a raspberry vinaigrette to dress this simple green salad. A lemon vinaigrette would also work well: substitute a lemon-infused olive oil for the sunflower oil.

Per serving
*1932 kJ, 461 kcal, 7 g protein, 46 g fat
(8 g saturated fat), 5 g carbohydrate
(4 g sugars), 5 g fibre, 6 mg sodium*

Gnocchi salad with pesto dressing

The gnocchi can be substituted with any cooked small pasta shapes. Substitute the capsicum and tomatoes with a jar of mixed vegetable antipasti to save time preparing and cooking the vegetables.

PREPARATION 20 minutes
COOKING 10 minutes
SERVES 4

400 g (14 oz) fresh small gnocchi

¼ cup (60 ml) olive oil

1 yellow capsicum (bell pepper), chopped

2 teaspoons brown sugar

1½ tablespoons white balsamic vinegar

200 g (7 oz) red cherry tomatoes

200 g (7 oz) marinated button mushrooms in oil

1 tablespoon pesto

freshly ground black pepper

⅓ cup (50 g) pitted black olives

150 g (5 oz) bocconcini (fresh baby mozzarella balls)

salt

1 Cook the gnocchi in a large saucepan of boiling water according to the packet instructions. Drain, briefly rinse under cold water and drain again.

2 While the gnocchi is cooking, heat half the oil in a frying pan over high heat. Cook the capsicum for 2 minutes, until starting to soften. Sprinkle with 1 teaspoon of the brown sugar and briefly cook until caramelised. Remove from the heat and drizzle the capsicum with half the vinegar. Pour the capsicum and juices into a large salad bowl.

3 Add 3 teaspoons of the oil to the pan and cook the whole tomatoes for 2 minutes, until they burst and release some of their juices. Sprinkle with the remaining brown sugar, briefly cook until caramelised and then drizzle with the remaining vinegar.

4 Add the tomatoes and juices to the capsicum, then add the mushrooms, pesto and the remaining oil. Toss to combine. Season with freshly ground black pepper.

5 Fold the gnocchi, olives and bocconcini through the capsicum mixture. Season again with salt and freshly ground black pepper. Set aside for at least 15 minutes before serving for the flavours to develop, if possible.

Per serving
1781 kJ, 425 kcal, 13 g protein, 24 g fat (7 g saturated fat), 38 g carbohydrate (6 g sugars), 3 g fibre, 607 mg sodium

Herbed Thai salad

This salad is based on larb, a Thai salad that combines minced or shredded chicken or beef with ginger, garlic, lime juice and plenty of herbs to make a high-protein light meal.

PREPARATION 20 minutes,
  plus 15 minutes cooling
COOKING 10 minutes
SERVES 4

1½ tablespoons light olive oil

500 g (1 lb) lean chicken or beef mince

2 teaspoons finely grated fresh ginger

2 cloves garlic, crushed

2 long green chillies, seeded and finely chopped

1 large French shallot, halved and thinly sliced

⅓ cup (10 g) fresh coriander (cilantro) leaves

2 tablespoons torn fresh mint

¼ cup (15 g) firmly packed torn fresh basil

1 kaffir lime (makrut) leaf, finely shredded

¼ cup (60 ml) lime juice

2 teaspoons fish sauce

1 tablespoon grated palm sugar, jaggery, dark brown sugar or caster (superfine) sugar

8 lettuce leaves, such as iceberg or butter lettuce, to serve

¼ cup (40 g) chopped unsalted roasted peanuts (groundnuts), to serve

1 Heat the oil in a wok or large frying pan over high heat. Add the chicken or beef, ginger, garlic and chillies, and stir to break up any lumps in the meat. Cook, stirring regularly, for 5 minutes, until just cooked through. Add the shallot and mix well. Transfer the mixture to a bowl and leave to cool for 15 minutes.

2 Add the coriander, mint and basil to the meat in the bowl. Put the kaffir lime leaf, lime juice, fish sauce and sugar in a small bowl and whisk to combine. Pour over the meat and herb mixture, and toss well.

3 Divide the lettuce leaves among four serving plates and fill with the meat and herb mixture. Sprinkle with the peanuts and serve.

If available, use Vietnamese mint and Thai basil instead of regular mint and basil for a more fragrant and authentic flavour. Fish sauce, known as nam pla in Thailand and nuoc nam in Vietnam, is available from Asian food stores and large supermarkets.

Per serving
1375 kJ, 328 kcal, 27 g protein, 22 g fat
(4 g saturated fat), 6 g carbohydrate
(4 g sugars), 2 g fibre, 336 mg sodium

Asian broccoli salad

Tiny florets of broccoli, baby corn and sugarsnap peas are briefly blanched and then tossed with crunchy raw vegetables in a soy and peanut butter dressing in this vegetarian salad. Toasted kasha adds a nutty flavour.

PREPARATION 20 minutes

COOKING 10 minutes

SERVES 4

2 tablespoons kasha (buckwheat grain)

300 g (10 oz) small broccoli florets

200 g (10 oz) small sugarsnap peas

125 g (4 oz) baby corn, halved lengthwise

8–10 spring onions (scallions), shredded

1 red capsicum (bell pepper), diced

100 g (3½ oz) baby bok choy leaves, halved lengthwise if large

1 cup (90 g) bean sprouts, trimmed

Peanut butter dressing

⅓ cup (90 g) crunchy peanut butter

100 ml (3½ fl oz) warm water

juice of 1 lemon

2 tablespoons light soy sauce

¼ teaspoon caster (superfine) sugar

1 teaspoon finely grated fresh ginger

1 Toast the kasha in a dry heavy-based frying pan over medium heat, stirring and tossing, for 4–5 minutes, until it has become slightly darker in colour. Remove from the heat and set aside.

2 To make the dressing, whisk all the ingredients together in a large salad bowl.

3 Bring a large saucepan of water to a boil. Add the broccoli florets, sugarsnap peas and baby corn to the boiling water and cook for 2 minutes, until the vegetables are slightly softened, but still crisp. Drain and refresh under cold running water.

4 Add the blanched vegetables to the salad bowl along with the spring onions, capsicum, bok choy and bean sprouts. Toss well to coat with the dressing. Serve immediately, with the kasha to be sprinkled over the top.

Per serving
*1001 kJ, 239 kcal, 14 g protein, 13 g fat
(2 g saturated fat), 16 g carbohydrate
(7 g sugars), 8 g fibre, 537 mg sodium*

Asparagus, snow pea and tomato salad with ginger dressing

This salad makes a lovely first course before grilled chicken and corn on the cob. It is an excellent source of folate, beta-carotene and vitamin C, key nutrients for fighting cancer and heart disease. Serve wedges of chilled watermelon for a refreshing dessert.

PREPARATION 10 minutes

COOKING 10 minutes

SERVES 6

125 g (4 oz) snow peas (mangetout), trimmed

500 g (1 lb) thin asparagus spears, trimmed

1 cos (romaine) lettuce, leaves separated

4 roma (plum) tomatoes, cut into wedges

¼ cup (25 g) toasted walnuts, coarsely chopped

Ginger dressing

1 tablespoon soy sauce

2 teaspoons rice vinegar

2 teaspoons lemon juice

1 teaspoon dark sesame oil

¼ cup (60 ml) vegetable oil

2 spring onions (scallions), finely chopped

1 tablespoon finely chopped fresh ginger

1 To make the dressing, whisk the soy sauce, rice vinegar, lemon juice and sesame oil in a small bowl. Whisk in the vegetable oil, then stir in the spring onions and ginger.

2 Cook the snow peas in a large saucepan of boiling water for 2–3 minutes, until tender but still crisp. Transfer to a colander with a slotted spoon, then rinse under cold running water.

3 Add the asparagus to the boiling water and cook for 3–4 minutes, until tender but still crisp. Drain in the colander, then rinse under cold running water. Toss the snow peas and asparagus in a large bowl with just enough dressing to lightly coat.

4 Arrange three or four lettuce leaves on each serving plate. Top with the snow peas, asparagus and tomatoes, and sprinkle the walnuts over the top. Serve the remaining dressing on the side.

Per serving
662 kJ, 158 kcal, 5 g protein, 13 g fat (1 g saturated fat), 5 g carbohydrate, (4 g sugars), 4 g fibre, 238 mg sodium

Prawn, peach and snow pea salad

If time permits, cook your own raw prawns. Cook them whole in a saucepan of gently boiling salted water for 3 minutes, until the flesh turns white. Alternatively, peel and chargrill the prawns.

PREPARATION 10 minutes
SERVES 4

250 g (8 oz) snow peas (mangetout), halved diagonally

2 peaches

500 g (1 lb) cooked, peeled prawns (shrimp), tails intact

8 cos (romaine) lettuce leaves

Lime dressing

2 tablespoons lime juice

¼ cup (60 ml) extra virgin olive oil

salt

freshly ground black pepper

1. Place the snow peas in a heatproof bowl and cover with boiling water. Leave for 1–2 minutes, until just softened. Drain and refresh under cold running water, then drain again and place in a large salad bowl.

2. Peel, halve and dice the peaches. Add to the snow peas, along with the prawns.

3. To make the dressing, whisk the lime juice with the oil and some salt and freshly ground black pepper.

4. Pour the dressing over the salad and gently mix to coat. Arrange the lettuce leaves on a serving platter. Pile the salad on top of the leaves and serve.

Add chopped fresh coriander (cilantro) or mint, or a chopped red chilli for extra bite. Substitute diced mango or avocado for the peaches, and swap the snow peas with snow pea sprouts. Instead of prawns, use other cooked crustaceans such as crayfish or lobster tails, or a combination.

Per serving
748 kJ, 178 kcal, 28 g protein, 2 g fat (<1 g saturated fat), 10 g carbohydrate (6 g sugars), 3 g fibre, 190 mg sodium

Pasta salad with basil and pancetta

This recipe is ideal for turning left-over pasta into a quick and easy salad. Briefly warm cold pasta in the microwave before tossing with the dressing to ensure that the pasta absorbs the dressing well.

PREPARATION 25 minutes,
 plus 1 hour marinating
COOKING 15 minutes
SERVES 4

300 g (10 oz) small pasta shells or other small pasta shapes

85 g (3 oz) pancetta, cut into thin strips

100 g (3½ oz) tomatoes, seeded and chopped

8–12 large fresh basil leaves, cut into strips

Balsamic dressing

1½ tablespoons red wine vinegar

2 teaspoons balsamic glaze

salt

freshly ground black pepper

⅓ cup (80 ml) olive oil

1 Add the pasta to a large saucepan of boiling water and cook according to the packet instructions, until al dente. Drain in a colander, briefly rinse with cold water and then drain again before tipping into a salad bowl.

2 While the pasta is cooking, heat a non-stick frying pan over medium heat and gently fry the pancetta strips for 2–3 minutes, until cooked but not browned.

3 To make the dressing, blend the red wine vinegar with the balsamic glaze. Season well with salt and freshly ground black pepper, then whisk in the olive oil.

4 Toss the warm pasta with the dressing, then fold in the tomatoes, pancetta and basil. Serve immediately, or set aside to marinate for 1 hour, if possible.

Pancetta is a salt-cured, seasoned Italian bacon, which can be easily replaced by any other streaky bacon. If you like, add some shaved parmesan to the salad just before serving. Balsamic glaze is a thick and sweet balsamic vinegar reduction. If not available, leave it out or replace with balsamic vinegar.

Per serving
1924 kJ, 460 kcal, 13 g protein, 22 g fat (4 g saturated fat), 52 g carbohydrate (<1 g sugars), 3 g fibre, 449 mg sodium

Bean salad

You can use just one type of canned bean if you like, such as cannellini beans or even chickpeas. Adding 2 teaspoons of chopped fresh rosemary will enhance the flavour of the salad.

PREPARATION 15 minutes,
  plus 30 minutes standing
COOKING 5 minutes
SERVES 6

200 g (7 oz) green beans, trimmed

420 g (15 oz) can four-bean mix, rinsed and drained

½ small red onion, thinly sliced

200 g (7 oz) baby roma (plum) or cherry tomatoes, halved

¼ cup (15 g) roughly chopped fresh parsley

2 tablespoons olive oil

1 tablespoon red wine vinegar

pinch of sugar

salt

freshly ground black pepper

1 Bring a saucepan of water to a boil. Add the green beans, cover and bring back to a boil, then remove the lid and cook for 2 minutes. Drain the beans and plunge into iced water to stop them cooking, then drain well. Cut the beans into thirds and place in a salad bowl.

2 Add the canned beans, red onion, tomatoes and parsley to the bowl. Add the oil, vinegar and sugar, and season with salt and freshly ground black pepper. Gently toss to combine.

3 Cover and stand at room temperature for 30 minutes to allow the flavours to develop before serving.

If you are preparing the salad ahead, cover and refrigerate it until needed, then return it to room temperature before serving.

Per serving
429 kJ, 102 kcal, 4 g protein, 6 g fat (<1 g saturated fat), 8 g carbohydrate (2 g sugars), 4 g fibre, 236 mg sodium

5 Quick lunch-box ideas

Preparing your own salads is a quick and easy way to make sure you eat a healthy lunch, as well as saving money. Use an insulated cooler bag with an ice brick to transport your salad so that it remains fresh and chilled until lunchtime.

Pitas with turkey and papaya salad

PREPARATION 10 minutes • COOKING 10 minutes • SERVES 4

Stir ⅔ **cup (160 g) Greek-style yogurt** and the finely grated zest and juice of ½ **lime** in a small bowl, and season with mild **curry powder** and **cayenne pepper.** Halve **2 Lebanese or other small cucumbers** lengthwise, scrape out the seeds and thinly slice. Peel, seed and slice ½ **ripe papaya.** Heat **1 tablespoon vegetable oil** in a small frying pan and cook **150 g (5 oz) turkey breast strips** over medium heat for 5–10 minutes, until golden. Fill **4 pita pockets** with the turkey, papaya and cucumber; wrap and chill until serving time. Add the dressing just before serving, along with a sprinkle of **curry powder,** if desired.

Per serving *1655 kJ, 395 kcal, 18 g protein, 11 g fat (4 g saturated fat), 55 g carbohydrate (14 g sugars), 5 g fibre, 448 mg sodium*

Tuna salad sandwiches

PREPARATION 10 minutes • SERVES 2

Peel ½ **Lebanese or other small cucumber** into thin strips. Combine ¼ **cup (60 g) low-fat natural (plain) yogurt, 5 finely chopped sprigs fresh flat-leaf parsley** and **2 teaspoons finely grated lemon zest** in a bowl. Season with **salt and freshly ground black pepper.** Drain and flake a **185 g (6 oz) can tuna in springwater,** and fold into the yogurt mixture. Chill until serving time. To assemble, place **4 thick slices wholegrain bread** on a board. Spread the tuna mixture on two of the slices, top with the cucumber and ½ **cup (25 g) baby spinach leaves,** and sprinkle with black pepper. Top with the remaining bread slices.

Per serving *1273 kJ, 304 kcal, 32 g protein, 7 g fat (2 g saturated fat), 23 g carbohydrate (4 g sugars), 12 g fibre, 609 mg sodium*

Pitas with turkey and papaya salad

Noodle salad

PREPARATION 10 minutes • COOKING 10 minutes • SERVES 2

Chargrill or barbecue **250 g (8 oz) rump (round) steak** to your liking; rest for 5 minutes, then thinly slice. Prepare **100 g (3½ oz) dried rice noodles** according to the packet instructions. Rinse with cold water and drain well. Toss the noodles and steak with **1 cup (150 g) mixed salad leaves, 8 blanched snow peas (mangetout), 1 grated carrot** and **100 g (3½ oz) quartered red cherry tomatoes.** Divide the salad between two containers and chill until serving time. Just before serving, toss with **2 tablespoons sweet chilli sauce** mixed with **lime juice,** to taste.

Per serving *1774 kJ, 424 kcal, 32 g protein, 6 g fat (3 g saturated fat), 60 g carbohydrate (12 g sugars), 5 g fibre, 573 mg sodium*

Chicken waldorf salad

PREPARATION 10 minutes • SERVES 2

Stir **1–2 teaspoons lemon juice** into ½ **cup (125 g) mayonnaise.** Toss **1 cup (175 g) shredded cooked chicken** with **1 thinly sliced red apple, 1 sliced stalk celery, 1 tablespoon chopped toasted walnuts** and **6 sliced baby cos (romaine) lettuce leaves** in a large bowl. Divide between two containers and chill until serving time. Add the dressing just before serving and toss to coat.

Per serving *1931 kJ, 461 kcal, 26 g protein, 30 g fat (5 g saturated fat), 22 g carbohydrate (18 g sugars), 3 g fibre, 588 mg sodium*

Prawn and potato salad

PREPARATION 10 minutes • COOKING 10 minutes • SERVES 2

Cook **500 g (1 lb) halved small new potatoes** in boiling water for 10 minutes, until tender. Drain and cool completely. Toss the potatoes with **1 tablespoon olive oil** and **1½ tablespoons white wine vinegar** or **lemon juice.** Add **1 cup (45 g) baby spinach leaves, 250 g (8 oz) cooked peeled prawns (shrimp), 100 g (3½ oz) halved red cherry tomatoes** and **2 sliced spring onions (scallions).** Divide the salad between two containers and chill until serving time.

Per serving *1599 kJ, 382 kcal, 34 g protein, 11 g fat (2 g saturated fat), 35 g carbohydrate (3 g sugars), 6 g fibre, 532 mg sodium*

Summer

Long, hot summer days are ideal for al fresco dining and cool salads, served either as main meals or as accompaniments to barbecued meats, chicken and seafood. Enjoy tomatoes, fennel and cucumbers, as well as stone fruits, figs, pineapple, watermelon and berries.

Greek salad with tahini dressing

Tahini, a Middle Eastern paste made of ground roasted sesame seeds, adds nutty flavour and creamy texture to the dressing of this salad. Serve it with crusty seeded bread for a light lunch or as a side dish.

PREPARATION 20 minutes
SERVES 4

200 g (7 oz) fetta

1 small cos (romaine) lettuce, torn into bite-sized pieces

½ cucumber, halved lengthwise and sliced

350 g (12 oz) large roma (plum) or other well-flavoured ripe tomatoes, sliced

1 small red onion, halved and thinly sliced

20 pitted kalamata olives

Tahini dressing

¼ cup (60 ml) extra virgin olive oil

1 tablespoon tahini

1 tablespoon lemon juice

freshly ground black pepper

4 large sprigs fresh flat-leaf parsley

1 Drain off any liquid from the fetta. Place the fetta in a small bowl of cold water to soak for a few minutes to remove the excess salt.

2 Meanwhile, divide the lettuce among four serving plates, then top with the cucumber, tomatoes and onion. Scatter the olives over the top.

3 To make the dressing, whisk the oil, tahini, lemon juice and a little freshly ground black pepper in a bowl. Use a pair of scissors to snip the parsley into the dressing.

4 Drain the fetta and crumble it into small pieces. Scatter about two-thirds of the fetta over the salads. Drizzle with the dressing, then scatter with the remaining fetta. Serve at room temperature.

In Greece, wild purslane, which has a mild taste and crunchy texture, is often used instead of the cos lettuce. Rocket (arugula) leaves, although more peppery in flavour, are another good substitute.

Per serving
1392 kJ, 333 kcal, 12 g protein, 30 g fat (10 g saturated fat), 4 g carbohydrate (3 g sugars), 3 g fibre, 770 mg sodium

Panzanella salad with chicken

Pan-fried chicken makes this Italian bread salad into a light meal. Buy roasted capsicums in a jar from the supermarket or from a delicatessen.

PREPARATION 10 minutes
COOKING 15 minutes
SERVES 2

2 thick slices day-old sourdough bread, about 110 g (3½ oz)

1 tablespoon olive oil

4 chicken tenderloins (tenders)

salt

freshly ground black pepper

½ roasted red capsicum (bell pepper), chopped

16 red cherry tomatoes, halved

12 pitted kalamata olives

24 small fresh basil leaves

Dressing

2 tablespoons olive oil

1½ tablespoons red wine vinegar

salt

freshly ground black pepper

1 Cut the bread into 2.5 cm (1 inch) cubes. Heat 3 teaspoons of the oil in a small non-stick frying pan over medium heat. Cook the bread cubes, turning often, for 4–5 minutes, until crisp and golden brown all over. Wipe the pan clean with paper towel.

2 Heat the remaining oil in the pan over medium–high heat. Season the chicken with salt and freshly ground black pepper, then cook for 4 minutes on each side, until cooked through. Cut the cooked chicken into thick slices.

3 Combine the capsicum, tomatoes, olives, basil and bread cubes in a bowl.

4 To make the dressing, whisk the oil with the vinegar and season with salt and freshly ground black pepper.

5 Pour the dressing over the salad and toss to combine. Add the chicken and lightly toss. Spoon the salad onto plates and serve immediately.

Per serving
*3147 kJ, 751 kcal, 47 g protein, 53 g fat
(9 g saturated fat), 22 g carbohydrate
(4 g sugars), 3 g fibre, 618 mg sodium*

Fattoush

This Middle Eastern bread salad is one of many frugal peasant dishes around the world that use bread (often stale bread) to add bulk and texture. Instead of baking, try frying the pita bread in a little olive oil until crisp.

PREPARATION 20 minutes
COOKING 15 minutes
SERVES 4

4 pitas, cut into quarters

1 tablespoon olive oil

1 tablespoon ground sumac

500 g (1 lb) baby roma (plum) tomatoes, halved

2 Lebanese or other small cucumbers, quartered lengthwise and chopped

1 red onion, halved and thinly sliced

⅓ cup (20 g) finely chopped fresh coriander (cilantro) leaves

⅓ cup (20 g) finely chopped fresh mint

½ cup (15 g) finely chopped fresh flat-leaf parsley

12 butter lettuce leaves, torn in half

150 g (5 oz) fetta, crumbled

75 g (2½ oz) kalamata olives

Sumac dressing

½ cup (125 ml) olive oil

¼ cup (60 ml) lemon juice

1 clove garlic, crushed

¼ teaspoon ground sumac

pinch of sea salt

1 Preheat the oven to 180°C (350°F/Gas 4). Lightly brush the pita quarters with the olive oil and sprinkle with the sumac. Place on a baking tray and bake for 10–15 minutes, until golden and crisp. Set aside to cool.

2 To make the dressing, whisk the oil, lemon juice, garlic, sumac and salt in a small bowl until well combined.

3 Combine the remaining ingredients in a large salad bowl. Tear or cut the cooled pita quarters into small pieces and add them to the bowl.

4 Pour the dressing over the salad, gently toss and serve.

Sumac is a dark purplish-red ground spice with a slightly sour, lemon taste. It is used in Lebanese dishes such as this bread salad.

Per serving
2867 kJ, 685 kcal, 17 g protein, 46 g fat (11 g saturated fat), 52 g carbohydrate (6 g sugars), 5 g fibre, 1189 mg sodium

Pistachio and goat's cheese salad

This Middle Eastern-inspired salad uses pistachios, which, like other nuts, are an excellent source of good fats. Briefly toast the pistachios in a dry frying pan for a more intense flavour.

PREPARATION 10 minutes
SERVES 4

4 large tomatoes, sliced into rounds

2 Lebanese or other small cucumbers, sliced into rounds

½ small red onion, thinly sliced into rounds

½ cup (10 g) fresh mint leaves (from about 4–6 sprigs)

⅓ cup (50 g) pistachios

100–150 g (3½–5 oz) goat's cheese

2 tablespoons extra virgin olive oil

juice of ½ lemon

1 teaspoon ground sumac

freshly ground black pepper

1 Layer the tomatoes, cucumbers, onion, mint leaves and pistachios on four individual serving plates. Alternatively, dice the tomatoes, cucumbers and onion, and toss in a large bowl with the mint leaves and pistachios.

2 Crumble the goat's cheese over the salads, then drizzle with the oil and lemon juice.

3 Sprinkle the sumac and freshly ground black pepper over the salad, and serve immediately.

If you don't like raw onion, try briefly cooking it in a little oil in a non-stick frying pan, and allowing it to cool before adding to the salad.

Per serving
1095 kJ, 261 kcal, 10 g protein, 22 g fat (7 g saturated fat), 7 g carbohydrate (6 g sugars), 4 g fibre, 152 mg sodium

Easy niçoise salad

PREPARATION 10 minutes
COOKING 10 minutes
SERVES 4

4 eggs

2 x 425 g (15 oz) cans chunky tuna
  in olive oil

2 baby cos (romaine) lettuces,
  leaves separated

½ cup (95 g) kalamata olives

2 tablespoons red wine vinegar

salt

freshly ground black pepper

Add some halved, steamed small new potatoes to the salad with some blanched green beans and red cherry tomato halves.

1 Put the eggs in a small saucepan, cover with cold water and bring to a boil over high heat. Reduce the heat and gently boil for 7 minutes, stirring occasionally. Drain the eggs and cool under cold running water. Leave to cool, then peel and cut into quarters.

2 Drain the tuna, reserving the oil. Arrange the lettuce, tuna, olives and egg quarters in a large salad bowl.

3 Whisk the vinegar with 2 tablespoons of the reserved tuna oil (add some extra virgin olive oil if needed) and some salt and freshly ground black pepper.

4 Pour the dressing over the salad, toss together and serve.

Per serving
*2067 kJ, 494 kcal, 49 g protein, 32 g fat
(6 g saturated fat), 3 g carbohydrate
(<1 g sugars), <1 g fibre, 1076 mg sodium*

Bocconcini and tomato salad

PREPARATION 10 minutes
SERVES 4

400 g (14 oz) tomatoes, sliced

300 g (10 oz) bocconcini (fresh baby mozzarella balls), sliced

16 fresh basil leaves

¼ cup (40 g) toasted pine nuts

Balsamic vinaigrette

2 tablespoons extra virgin olive oil

1½ tablespoons balsamic vinegar

salt

freshly ground black pepper

1 Arrange the tomato and bocconcini slices on a large serving plate.

2 Roughly tear the basil leaves. Scatter the basil and pine nuts over the salad.

3 To make the vinaigrette, whisk the oil with the vinegar and some salt and freshly ground black pepper.

4 Drizzle the vinaigrette over the salad and serve with crusty bread as a light first course.

You can toast pine nuts by tossing them in a dry frying pan over medium heat for 2–3 minutes, until golden.

Per serving
*1010 kJ, 241 kcal, 15 g protein, 18 g fat
(8 g saturated fat), 3 g carbohydrate
(3 g sugars), 2 g fibre, 216 mg sodium*

Apple and fennel salad with toasted hazelnuts

For a more substantial salad, add some barbecued or smoked chicken. Use green apples, or use half a green one and half a red one, leaving the skin on for extra colour. Walnuts would also go well with the apple and fennel.

PREPARATION 10 minutes
SERVES 4

2 small bulbs fennel, about 225 g (8 oz) each, with fronds

1 large red apple

2 cups (60 g) watercress sprigs

⅓ cup (45 g) toasted hazelnuts

Lemon dressing

¼ cup (60 ml) extra virgin olive oil

2 tablespoons lemon juice

salt

freshly ground black pepper

1 Trim the root end from the fennel bulbs, reserving the fronds as a garnish. Cut the fennel bulbs into quarters, then thinly slice and place in a large salad bowl.

2 Cut the apple into quarters and remove the core. Thinly slice the apple quarters, leaving the skin on. Add to the fennel with the watercress and hazelnuts.

3 To make the dressing, whisk the oil with the lemon juice and some salt and freshly ground black pepper.

4 Drizzle the dressing over the salad and toss well. Serve garnished with the reserved fennel fronds.

Toasted hazelnuts are available from some supermarkets, but it is easy to toast your own. Place the nuts in a frying pan without any oil and fry over medium heat, stirring occasionally, until golden. Wrap in a clean cloth and rub to remove the papery skins.

Per serving
520 kJ, 124 kcal, 4 g protein, 7 g fat (<1 g saturated fat), 11 g carbohydrate (11 g sugars), 6 g fibre, 51 mg sodium

Middle Eastern salad

Lots of chopped fresh herbs give this quick and simple dish its pronounced flavour, and bite-sized pieces of crisp, toasted pita bread provide texture. Serve the salad for a light meal with a hint of summer at any time of year.

PREPARATION 15 minutes

COOKING 2 minutes

SERVES 4

2 large white or sesame seed pitas

½ Lebanese or other small cucumber, finely chopped

4 large tomatoes, finely chopped

4 spring onions (scallions), thinly sliced on the diagonal

400 g (14 oz) can chickpeas or black-eyed peas, rinsed and drained

fresh mint leaves, to garnish

Herb dressing

⅓ cup (80 ml) olive oil

juice of 1 lemon

salt

freshly ground black pepper

2 tablespoons chopped fresh coriander (cilantro)

2 tablespoons chopped fresh mint

1 Warm the pitas in the toaster for 1 minute to make them easier to open, then split each in half using a knife. Toast for 1 minute, until crisp and lightly browned. Tear the pitas into bite-sized pieces.

2 To make the dressing, whisk the oil and lemon juice in a small bowl. Season with salt and freshly ground black pepper, then stir in the coriander and mint.

3 Combine the cucumber, tomatoes, spring onions and chickpeas or black-eyed peas in a large bowl. Drizzle with the dressing, then toss until well mixed. Just before serving, gently mix through the pita pieces. Serve the salad garnished with mint leaves.

Serve the salad sprinkled with some sunflower seeds and crumbled goat's cheese for extra flavour and texture.

Per serving
1637 kJ, 391 kcal, 11 g protein, 20 g fat (3 g saturated fat), 41 g carbohydrate (6 g sugars), 7 g fibre, 587 mg sodium

Tofu and papaya noodle salad

Serve this Asian-style salad with barbecued salmon, tuna, beef or chicken. Replace the rice noodles with rice vermicelli or cellophane noodles.

PREPARATION 10 minutes,
  plus 5 minutes soaking
SERVES 4

200 g (7 oz) dried thin or thick rice noodles

500 g (1 lb) papaya or mango

200 g (7 oz) marinated tofu with Thai flavourings, thinly sliced

2 tablespoons chopped fresh coriander (cilantro) or mint

Soy dressing

¼ cup (60 ml) soy sauce

1 tablespoon sesame oil

1 Place the noodles in a large heatproof bowl. Cover with boiling water and soak for 5 minutes, until the noodles have softened, then drain well. Using scissors, snip the noodles into thirds, then place in a large salad bowl.

2 While the noodles are soaking, peel and dice the papaya or mango, removing the seeds or stone.

3 To make the dressing, whisk the soy sauce with the sesame oil in a small bowl.

4 Add the papaya or mango, tofu, coriander or mint and the dressing to the noodles. Toss well and serve.

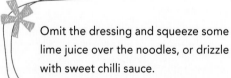

Omit the dressing and squeeze some lime juice over the noodles, or drizzle with sweet chilli sauce.

Per serving
1416 kJ, 338 kcal, 13 g protein, 6 g fat
(1 g saturated fat), 57 g carbohydrate
(8 g sugars), 3 g fibre, 1536 mg sodium

Tabouleh

This traditional Middle Eastern salad is made using burghul, also known as bulgur – hulled wheat that has been dried and steamed, so it cooks in a relatively short time.

PREPARATION 25 minutes
COOKING 15 minutes
SERVES 4

200 g (7 oz) burghul (bulgur)

1 bunch (150 g/5 oz) fresh flat-leaf parsley

8 large fresh peppermint or mint leaves, plus extra to garnish

2 cloves garlic

300 g (10 oz) tomatoes, diced

lemon slices, to serve

Lemon dressing

¼ cup (60 ml) olive oil

2 tablespoons lemon juice

pinch of salt

freshly ground black pepper

1 Cook the burghul according to the packet instructions. Spread the hot burghul out on a plate to allow the moisture to evaporate, or rinse in a colander with cold water and squeeze out any excess moisture.

2 Pick off the parsley leaves and place in a food processor with the peppermint or mint leaves. Add the garlic cloves and finely chop. Alternatively, use a large, sharp knife to chop the herbs and garlic. Add the herb mixture to a large salad bowl along with the tomatoes.

3 To make the dressing, whisk the oil with the lemon juice, salt and some freshly ground black pepper.

4 Add the dressing to the bowl with the tomatoes and herbs. Toss to combine, then mix in the burghul. Serve the salad with lemon slices, garnished with the extra peppermint or mint leaves.

Supermarkets stock different kinds of burghul, which often have different cooking times, so check the cooking instructions on the packet.

Per serving
1262 kJ, 301 kcal, 7 g protein, 15 g fat (2 g saturated fat), 32 g carbohydrate (2 g sugars), 9 g fibre, 182 mg sodium

Salmon and avocado noodle salad

These soba noodles are served cold, making a lovely meal for a
hot day. Sprinkle some toasted white or black sesame seeds over
the salad for a crunchy texture and nutty flavour.

PREPARATION 10 minutes
COOKING 10 minutes
SERVES 4

270 g (9½ oz) packet soba noodles

2 teaspoons vegetable oil

2 x 250 g (8 oz) salmon fillets, skin
removed

2 tablespoons ponzu sauce

4 spring onions (scallions), thinly sliced

1 avocado, diced

1 Add the noodles to a saucepan of boiling water. Cover
and bring back to a boil, then remove the lid and cook
for 4 minutes, until tender. Drain in a colander, then
rinse under cold running water. Set aside to drain.

2 Meanwhile, heat the oil in a non-stick frying pan over
medium heat. Add the salmon and cook for 3 minutes
on each side, until just cooked through. Allow to cool
slightly, then flake into chunks.

3 Put the noodles in a large serving bowl and drizzle
with the ponzu sauce. Add the spring onions, salmon
and avocado, and gently toss to combine. Serve the
salad immediately.

Ponzu sauce is a Japanese sauce used
for dipping or dressing. It is available
from large supermarkets and specialty
food stores. If you can't find it, use soy
sauce mixed with lemon juice.

Per serving
*2363 kJ, 564 kcal, 34 g protein, 24 g fat
(5 g saturated fat), 52 g carbohydrate
(2 g sugars), 3 g fibre, 789 mg sodium*

Seared tuna, egg and olive salad

We've used sashimi-quality tuna steaks here, but you can also use canned sliced tuna. Arrange the tuna slices on the salad and generously season with freshly ground black pepper.

PREPARATION 30 minutes
COOKING 15 minutes
SERVES 4

2 sashimi-quality tuna steaks, about 150 g (5 oz) each

olive oil, for brushing

3 eggs

½ iceberg lettuce, shredded

100 g (3½ oz) red cherry tomatoes, halved

½ cucumber, quartered lengthwise and sliced

1 yellow capsicum (bell pepper), cut into strips

100 g (3½ oz) mixed pitted olives

3 teaspoons black peppercorns

1 teaspoon coriander seeds

1 teaspoon sea salt flakes (optional)

Mustard dressing

⅓ cup (80 ml) olive oil

¼ cup (60 ml) white wine vinegar

1–2 teaspoons dijon mustard

freshly ground black pepper

1 Rinse the tuna steaks under cold water, then pat dry. Brush the tuna with a little oil, cover and set aside.

2 Put the eggs in a small saucepan, cover with cold water and bring to a boil over high heat. Reduce the heat and gently boil for 7 minutes, stirring occasionally. Drain the eggs and cool under cold running water. Leave to cool, then peel and cut into quarters.

3 To make the dressing, add the oil, vinegar and mustard to a screw-top jar, and season with freshly ground black pepper. Shake until the ingredients are well combined.

4 Combine the lettuce, tomatoes, cucumber, capsicum and olives in a large bowl. Fold in the dressing. Divide the salad among four serving plates and arrange the egg quarters on top.

5 Using a mortar and pestle, grind the black peppercorns, coriander seeds and sea salt flakes, if using. Place the spice mixture on a plate.

6 Heat a non-stick frying pan over medium heat and cook the tuna for 2–3 minutes on each side, until seared on the outside but rare in the centre. Remove from the pan. Cut the tuna into cubes and roll in the ground spices.

7 Arrange the tuna on top of the salad and serve immediately.

Per serving
1621 kJ, 387 kcal, 25 g protein, 29 g fat (6 g saturated fat), 5 g carbohydrate (2 g sugars), 2 g fibre, 402 mg sodium

European potato salad

Potato salads are always popular and are very versatile. This version is layered with herbs and gherkins, and goes especially well with seafood and chicken for summer picnics.

PREPARATION 15 minutes
COOKING 15 minutes
SERVES 8

1 kg (2 lb) small new potatoes

¼ cup (60 ml) olive oil

¼ cup (60 ml) white wine vinegar

2 tablespoons chopped fresh parsley

2 tablespoons chopped fresh dill

½ red onion, finely chopped

¼ cup (45 g) finely chopped gherkins (pickles) or pickled cucumber

salt

freshly ground black pepper

1 Place the potatoes in a large saucepan and cover with cold water. Bring to a boil and cook for 10 minutes, until tender when pierced with a skewer. Drain and cool slightly, then cut into thick slices.

2 Layer one-third of the potatoes in a serving dish. Whisk together the olive oil and vinegar, and drizzle one-third over the potatoes. Reserve a little of the herbs for the top, then sprinkle half the remaining herbs over the potatoes, followed by half the onion and gherkins or cucumbers. Season well with salt and freshly ground black pepper.

3 Repeat the layers, finishing with the oil and vinegar, and seasoning each layer well. Sprinkle the reserved herbs over the salad and serve at room temperature.

You can use any boiling (or 'waxy') potatoes here, as distinct from baking (or 'floury') potatoes, which are more starchy and suited to baking. Boiling or waxy potatoes are often yellow-fleshed, and hold their shape well during cooking.

Per serving
611 kJ, 146 kcal, 3 g protein, 7 g fat (<1 g saturated fat), 17 g carbohydrate (<1 g sugars), 3 g fibre, 149 mg sodium

Prawns with rice salad and dill dressing

Seared prawns are served piled on a mixture of aromatic basmati and wild rice, crunchy broccoli florets, snow peas and yellow capsicum tossed in a fresh dill and lime juice dressing. Together the ingredients make a well-balanced main meal salad.

PREPARATION 15 minutes
COOKING 30 minutes
SERVES 4

1¼ cups (265 g) mixed basmati and wild rice, well rinsed

thinly pared zest and juice of 1 lime

¼ cup (60 ml) sunflower or vegetable oil

2 teaspoons sesame oil

1 tablespoon light soy sauce

salt

freshly ground black pepper

125 g (4 oz) broccoli, broken into small florets

125 g (4 oz) snow peas (mangetout), halved lengthwise

400 g (14 oz) raw prawns (uncooked shrimp), peeled, tails intact

1 small yellow capsicum (bell pepper), thinly sliced

3–4 spring onions (scallions), cut into short lengths

⅓ cup (20 g) coarsely chopped fresh dill

1 Bring a saucepan of water to a boil. Add the rice and lime zest, and cook for 20 minutes, or according to the packet instructions, until tender. Drain the rice and tip it into a wide salad bowl. Discard the lime zest.

2 Whisk 1 tablespoon of the lime juice with 2 tablespoons of the sunflower or vegetable oil, the sesame oil and the soy sauce in a small bowl. Season with salt and freshly ground black pepper. Drizzle the dressing over the rice and stir to combine. Spread out the rice in the bowl and leave to cool.

3 Meanwhile, steam the broccoli over a saucepan of boiling water for 4 minutes. Add the snow peas and steam for a further 2 minutes, until the vegetables are tender but still crisp. Tip the vegetables into a colander and refresh them under cold running water.

4 Heat the remaining oil in a large frying pan and cook the prawns over high heat for 1–2 minutes on each side, until pink and cooked through. Remove from the heat and sprinkle with the remaining lime juice.

5 Add the broccoli, snow peas, capsicum, spring onions and three-quarters of the dill to the rice and gently stir. Pile the prawns on top and sprinkle with the remaining dill. Serve immediately.

Per serving
2164 kJ, 517 kcal, 31 g protein, 19 g fat (2 g saturated fat), 56 g carbohydrate (4 g sugars), 5 g fibre, 887 mg sodium

Tossed leaf and herb salad

A leafy salad with plenty of fresh herbs makes an excellent accompaniment to a whole range of dishes, from a simple roasted chicken with potatoes, to pizza and pasta. For a crisp texture, make the salad just before you want to serve it and then toss with the dressing at the very last moment.

PREPARATION 10 minutes
SERVES 6

2 cos (romaine) lettuces, cut crosswise into thick slices
6 red coral lettuce leaves
¼ telegraph (long) cucumber, thinly sliced
12 large fresh basil leaves, roughly torn
1 tablespoon coarsely chopped fresh tarragon
5 large spring onions (scallions), thinly sliced

Mustard vinaigrette
¼ cup (60 ml) extra virgin olive oil
1 tablespoon red wine vinegar
½ teaspoon dijon mustard
pinch of caster (superfine) sugar (optional)
salt
freshly ground black pepper

1 Place the cos lettuce, red coral lettuce, cucumber, herbs and spring onions in a large salad bowl.

2 To make the vinaigrette, whisk the oil, vinegar, mustard and sugar, if using, in a bowl. Season with salt and freshly ground black pepper.

3 Just before serving, drizzle the vinaigrette over the salad and thoroughly toss until all the ingredients are lightly coated. Serve immediately.

Per serving
*385 kJ, 92 kcal, <1 g protein, 9 g fat
(1 g saturated fat), 2 g carbohydrate
(2 g sugars), <1 g fibre, 118 mg sodium*

Fig, prosciutto and blue cheese salad

PREPARATION 10 minutes
SERVES 4

6 figs
8 slices prosciutto
1⅓ cups (60 g) baby rocket (arugula)
60 g (2 oz) blue cheese
extra virgin olive oil, for drizzling
balsamic glaze, for drizzling
freshly ground black pepper

1 Cut the figs lengthwise into quarters. Tear each prosciutto slice into four to six pieces.

2 Arrange the rocket, fig quarters and prosciutto on four serving plates.

3 Crumble the blue cheese over the top of the salads, then drizzle with a little extra virgin olive oil and balsamic glaze. Sprinkle with freshly ground black pepper and serve.

This salad makes a lovely starter, or you could increase the quantities slightly and serve with crusty bread for lunch.

Balsamic glaze is a thick and sweet balsamic vinegar reduction. You'll find it in supermarkets, in the salad dressing aisle.

Per serving
684 kJ, 163 kcal, 11 g protein, 10 g fat
(6 g saturated fat), 7 g carbohydrate
(7 g sugars), 2 g fibre, 495 mg sodium

Curried chicken salad
with **spinach** and **nectarines**

Substitute the chicken with turkey or with firm tofu for a vegetarian version. If you like a bit more spice, replace the mild curry powder with a hot variety or add a finely chopped red chilli. Use papaya, mango or well-drained, canned peaches instead of nectarines.

PREPARATION 20 minutes
COOKING 10 minutes
SERVES 4

1½ tablespoons olive oil

400 g (14 oz) boneless, skinless chicken breasts, cut into thin strips

1½ tablespoons lemon juice

1 clove garlic, crushed

3 teaspoons mild curry powder

2 teaspoons soy sauce

freshly ground black pepper

50 g (1¾ oz) sugarsnap peas or snow peas (mangetout), trimmed

2 ripe, sweet nectarines

300 g (10 oz) natural (plain) yogurt

3 teaspoons mango chutney

1 teaspoon honey

2¼ cups (100 g) baby spinach leaves or rocket (arugula)

⅓ cup (30 g) toasted flaked almonds

1 Heat the oil in a frying pan and cook the chicken strips over medium heat for 4–5 minutes, until cooked through. Remove the pan from the heat.

2 Combine the lemon juice, garlic, curry powder and soy sauce in a small bowl. Season with freshly ground black pepper. Add the mixture to the pan and toss to coat the chicken. Set aside.

3 Blanch the sugarsnap peas or snow peas in a saucepan of boiling water for 2 minutes. Drain and briefly rinse under cold water. Cut in half on the diagonal if large.

4 Halve the nectarines and remove the stones. Cut three halves into thin wedges and dice the remainder.

5 Put the yogurt in a bowl and add the diced nectarines, chutney and 1 tablespoon of the curry mixture from the pan, leaving the chicken in the pan. Stir in the honey.

6 Divide the spinach or rocket leaves among four serving plates and arrange the chicken, sugarsnap peas or snow peas and nectarine wedges on top. Spoon the dressing over the salad and garnish with the flaked almonds.

Per serving
*1479 kJ, 353 kcal, 29 g protein, 19 g fat
(5 g saturated fat), 15 g carbohydrate
(14 g sugars), 4 g fibre, 311 mg sodium*

Ham and tomato pasta salad

Great for picnics, barbecues and lunch-boxes, pasta salads are versatile and easy to prepare ahead. For a smart twist, use prosciutto or thinly sliced salami instead of ham.

PREPARATION 15 minutes

COOKING 15 minutes

SERVES 4

300 g (10 oz) pasta spirals, or other short pasta, such as penne or farfalle

¼ cup (60 g) mayonnaise

3 teaspoons lemon juice

310 g (10 oz) can corn kernels, drained

1 carrot, grated

100 g (3½ oz) red cherry tomatoes, halved

150 g (5 oz) sliced ham, chopped

2 tablespoons finely chopped fresh parsley

1 Add the pasta to a large saucepan of boiling water and cook according to the packet instructions, until al dente. Drain in a colander, briefly rinse with cold water and then drain again before tipping into a salad bowl.

2 Add the mayonnaise and lemon juice to the pasta. Gently toss to combine.

3 Add the corn kernels, carrot, tomatoes, ham and parsley to the pasta, and toss again. Serve at room temperature, or cover and refrigerate until required.

Replace the vegetables and parsley with pitted black olives, roasted red capsicum (bell pepper), semi-dried (sun-blushed) tomatoes and fresh basil, and dress with olive oil and balsamic vinegar instead of the mayonnaise and lemon juice.

Per serving
1659 kJ, 396 kcal, 17 g protein, 8 g fat (1 g saturated fat), 64 g carbohydrate (5 g sugars), 5 g fibre, 814 mg sodium

Rice salad

On hot summer nights, a cool rice salad is the perfect partner for grilled or barbecued chicken or fish. The rice is speckled with diced raw vegetables for vibrant colour and a palate-pleasing crunch.

PREPARATION 20 minutes
COOKING 10 minutes
SERVES 8

1 cup (200 g) long-grain white rice

310 g (10 oz) can corn kernels, drained

4 spring onions (scallions), sliced

1 small red capsicum (bell pepper), diced

1 small Lebanese or other small cucumber, diced

2 stalks celery, thinly sliced

Dressing

¼ cup (60 ml) lemon juice

2 tablespoons olive oil

1 Cook the rice in a large saucepan of boiling water for 10 minutes, until just tender. Drain well. Leave to cool, turning the rice over occasionally with a large metal spoon to release the heat.

2 Once the rice has cooled to room temperature, fold in the corn kernels, spring onions, capsicum, cucumber and celery.

3 To make the dressing, whisk the lemon juice and oil in a small bowl.

4 Pour the dressing over the rice and gently fold until all the ingredients are coated. Serve the salad at room temperature, or cover and refrigerate until required.

Rice left unrefrigerated can pose a food poisoning risk. If not using it immediately, keep the rice covered in the fridge for no more than 1–2 days. Take it out 20 minutes before serving.

Per serving
672 kJ, 160 kcal, 3 g protein, 5 g fat (<1 g saturated fat), 26 g carbohydrate (2 g sugars), 2 g fibre, 78 mg sodium

Thai-style bok choy salad

This refreshing raw salad with its mildly spicy Thai flavours makes an ideal accompaniment to barbecued meat, poultry, fish or seafood.

PREPARATION 20 minutes
SERVES 4

2 baby bok choy

¼ pineapple, chopped

1 Lebanese or other small cucumber, seeded and diced

1 red onion, halved and thinly sliced

1 small handful fresh mint

1 small handful fresh Thai basil

Lime dressing

2 cloves garlic, crushed

3 teaspoons brown sugar

2 tablespoons lime juice

1½ tablespoons fish sauce

1½ tablespoons sweet chilli sauce

1½ tablespoons vegetable oil

pinch of salt (optional)

1 Cut the bok choy into strips about 1 cm (½ inch) wide, discarding the hard bottom section. Place the strips in a large bowl with the pineapple, cucumber and onion.

2 Cut any large mint and Thai basil leaves into strips, and leave smaller ones whole. Add the herbs to the bowl.

3 To make the dressing, put the garlic, sugar, lime juice, fish sauce, sweet chilli sauce, oil and salt, if using, in a small bowl. Whisk until thoroughly combined.

4 Just before serving, pour the dressing over the salad and gently mix to coat.

Dice some left-over cooked chicken or pork to add to the salad. Coat the meat in the dressing and allow it to marinate for at least 30 minutes, then add it to the salad together with the dressing just before serving.

Per serving
511 kJ, 122 kcal, 2 g protein, 7 g fat (<1 g saturated fat), 13 g carbohydrate (9 g sugars), 2 g fibre, 812 mg sodium

Prawn and noodle salad

This salad can be served as a refreshing first course or as a tasty accompaniment to grilled or barbecued chicken, turkey or fish. Substitute the rockmelon with other sweet, juicy fruits such as mango, papaya or pineapple.

PREPARATION 20 minutes, plus 10 minutes soaking

SERVES 4

100 g (3½ oz) dried rice vermicelli

3 spring onions (scallions)

¼ rockmelon (cantaloupe)

200 g (7 oz) cooked, peeled prawns (shrimp)

½ cucumber, seeded and diced

10 fresh mint leaves, cut into strips (optional)

Sweet chilli dressing

¼ cup (60 ml) vegetable oil

2 tablespoons sweet chilli sauce

1½ tablespoons lime juice

3 teaspoons mirin or sherry

freshly ground black pepper

1 tablespoon pickled ginger, drained and chopped

1. Soak the vermicelli in boiling water for 5–10 minutes, according to the packet instructions.

2. Meanwhile, trim the spring onions, removing the dark green parts. Halve the white and light green sections lengthwise, then cut into strips. Seed the rockmelon and remove the flesh using a melon baller.

3. To make the dressing, put the oil, sweet chilli sauce, lime juice and mirin or sherry in a large bowl. Season with freshly ground black pepper and whisk until well combined. Stir in the pickled ginger.

4. Rinse the prawns well under cold running water, then drain and pat dry with paper towel. Stir the prawns into the dressing, along with the spring onions, rockmelon and cucumber.

5. Drain the vermicelli and cut into manageable lengths using kitchen scissors. Add to the bowl with the other ingredients and toss to combine. Serve topped with the shredded mint, if using.

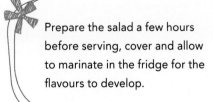

Prepare the salad a few hours before serving, cover and allow to marinate in the fridge for the flavours to develop.

Per serving
1323 kJ, 316 kcal, 14 g protein, 15 g fat (2 g saturated fat), 32 g carbohydrate (8 g sugars), <1 g fibre, 547 mg sodium

Peach and cottage cheese salad

This fresh salad combines luscious, sweet peaches and crisp green vegetables with a generous portion of creamy cottage cheese. It is quick and easy to put together, taking only a little longer to make than a sandwich.

PREPARATION 20 minutes

COOKING 5 minutes

SERVES 4

1²⁄₃ cups (255 g) frozen broad (fava) beans

175 g (6 oz) snow peas (mangetout), halved

100 g (3½ oz) rocket (arugula)

50 g (1¾ oz) lamb's lettuce (mâche)

4 ripe peaches, cut into thin wedges

2 cups (500 g) cottage cheese

⅓ cup (30 g) toasted flaked almonds

cayenne pepper

fresh dill sprigs, to serve

Honey and dill dressing

2 tablespoons extra virgin olive oil

grated zest and juice of 1 lemon

1 teaspoon wholegrain or dijon mustard

2 teaspoons honey

2 tablespoons chopped fresh dill

salt

freshly ground black pepper

1 Plunge the broad beans into a saucepan of boiling water and cook for 4 minutes. Add the snow peas and cook for a further 1 minute. Drain the beans and snow peas in a sieve, and refresh under cold running water.

2 To make the dressing, put the oil, lemon zest and juice, mustard, honey and dill in a mixing bowl, and season with salt and freshly ground black pepper. Whisk well.

3 Add the beans, snow peas, rocket and lamb's lettuce to the bowl, and toss to coat with the dressing.

4 Divide the salad among four serving plates. Arrange the peach slices over the top and spoon on the cottage cheese. Sprinkle with the flaked almonds and a little cayenne pepper. Serve garnished with dill sprigs.

The fresh peaches can be replaced with fresh nectarines or with well-drained canned peaches.

Per serving
1669 kJ, 399 kcal, 29 g protein, 21 g fat (6 g saturated fat), 21 g carbohydrate (18 g sugars), 8 g fibre, 589 mg sodium

Mango chicken salad

Here is a very special salad – new potatoes, slices of tender chicken and asparagus tossed in a mellow fresh orange dressing and then gently mixed with juicy mango slices and baby salad leaves. It makes a lovely well-balanced meal all on its own.

PREPARATION 15 minutes,
  plus 15 minutes marinating
COOKING 35 minutes
SERVES 4

1 clove garlic, crushed

1 teaspoon grated fresh ginger

1 tablespoon light soy sauce

2 teaspoons sunflower or vegetable oil

2 boneless, skinless chicken breasts,
  about 175 g (6 oz) each

800 g (1¾ lb) new potatoes, scrubbed

2 large sprigs fresh mint

125 g (4 oz) asparagus spears, trimmed

1 ripe mango, sliced

150 g (5 oz) mixed baby salad leaves,
  such as baby spinach, cos (romaine)
  lettuce and red coral lettuces

Orange dressing

½ teaspoon finely grated orange zest

1 tablespoon orange juice

2 tablespoons sunflower or
  vegetable oil

1 tablespoon walnut oil

1 teaspoon dijon mustard

salt

freshly ground black pepper

1 Whisk the garlic, ginger, soy sauce and oil in a bowl. Add the chicken breasts and turn to coat both sides, then leave to marinate for 15 minutes.

2 Put the potatoes in a saucepan, cover with boiling water and add the mint sprigs. Cook for 15–20 minutes, until tender. At the same time, put the asparagus in a steamer basket or metal colander, cover and set over the pan of potatoes to steam. Cook thin asparagus spears for about 4 minutes, thick spears for about 8 minutes, until just tender. Drain the potatoes, discarding the mint. Leave until cool enough to handle, then cut into thick slices. Cut the asparagus into thick slices on the diagonal.

3 Preheat the grill (broiler) to medium. Place the marinated chicken on the grill rack. Grill (broil) for about 15 minutes, brushing frequently with the marinade and turning once, until cooked through and the juices run clear when the chicken is pierced with the tip of a knife. Leave to rest for 3–4 minutes, then slice.

4 To make the dressing, put the orange zest and juice, oils and mustard in a large serving bowl, and whisk together until slightly thickened. Season with salt and freshly ground black pepper.

5 Transfer the warm sliced chicken, potatoes and asparagus to the bowl and gently toss to coat with the dressing. Add the mango and salad leaves, and gently toss again. Serve immediately, while still warm.

Per serving
*1835 kJ, 438 kcal, 26 g protein, 21 g fat
(3 g saturated fat), 36 g carbohydrate
(10 g sugars), 6 g fibre, 434 mg sodium*

Watermelon, mint and labna salad

This light and refreshing Greek-style salad is best assembled close to serving time, although you need to begin preparing the labna 24 hours ahead. The dressing and watermelon can be prepared 2 hours ahead.

PREPARATION 20 minutes,
  plus 24 hours draining
SERVES 4

1.5 kg (3 lb) seedless watermelon, rind removed

½ small red onion, very thinly sliced, rings separated

¼ cup (5 g) fresh mint

Labna

2 cups (500 g) low-fat Greek-style yogurt

1½ teaspoons fine table salt

½ teaspoon freshly ground black pepper

1 clove garlic, crushed

Dressing

1 tablespoon extra virgin olive oil

1 tablespoon balsamic vinegar

freshly ground black pepper

1 To make the labna, rinse a 25 cm (10 inch) square of muslin (cheesecloth) in hot water. Wring out the muslin, then use it to line a mesh strainer and place over a bowl. Combine the yogurt, salt, pepper and garlic in a bowl, then spoon into the strainer and cover with plastic wrap. Refrigerate for at least 24 hours to drain.

2 Thinly slice the watermelon, then cut it into small wedges. Discard any visible seeds. Arrange the watermelon in a shallow serving bowl. Scatter the onion rings and all but a few mint leaves over the top.

3 To make the dressing, whisk the oil, balsamic vinegar and a good grinding of black pepper in a small bowl.

4 Drizzle the dressing over the salad. Turn the labna out onto a plate and remove the muslin. Crumble the labna over the salad. Scatter the remaining mint leaves over the top and serve.

Labna is a yogurt cheese that is easy to make at home. Alternatively, purchase it from specialty or health-food stores, or use soft goat's cheese instead.

Per serving
1140 kJ, 272 kcal, 11 g protein, 9 g fat (4 g saturated fat), 35 g carbohydrate (30 g sugars), 3 g fibre, 1104 mg sodium

Garden salad with creamy herb dressing

The quantities indicated in the recipe serve four for lunch or a light meal, accompanied by some crusty bread. If you are serving the salad as a side dish, halve the quantities. Save time by using packaged mixed lettuce leaves.

PREPARATION 20 minutes
SERVES 4

1 large frilly-edged lettuce, leaves separated

200 g (7 oz) carrots, thinly sliced

8 radishes, thinly sliced

200 g (7 oz) cucumber, thinly sliced

1 bunch (30 g/1 oz) fresh chives, snipped

Creamy herb dressing

1 cup (250 g) crème fraîche

⅓ cup (80 ml) light cream

1 tablespoon finely chopped fresh herbs, such as chervil, parsley and chives

1 tablespoon medium–hot mustard

1 Tear the lettuce leaves into bite-sized pieces and place in a large salad bowl or on individual plates.

2 Arrange the sliced carrots, radishes and cucumber over the lettuce.

3 To make the dressing, whisk the crème fraîche, cream, herbs and mustard in a small bowl until combined.

4 Spoon a little of the dressing over the salad, then sprinkle with the chives. Serve the remaining dressing on the side.

Using a mandolin to cut the vegetables will save time and help you achieve very thin, uniform slices.

Per serving
1503 kJ, 359 kcal, 4 g protein, 35 g fat (25 g saturated fat), 8 g carbohydrate (7 g sugars), 3 g fibre, 183 mg sodium

Corn and tomato salad

PREPARATION 20 minutes
SERVES 4

310 g (10 oz) can corn kernels, rinsed and drained

1 green capsicum (bell pepper), cut into strips

2 tomatoes, chopped

2 stalks celery, thinly sliced

1 red onion, halved and thinly sliced

fresh coriander (cilantro) sprigs, to garnish

Dressing

¼ cup (60 ml) olive oil

2 tablespoons lime juice

1 tablespoon white wine vinegar

1 teaspoon brown sugar

½ teaspoon ground cumin

large pinch of cayenne pepper

1 clove garlic, crushed

1 tablespoon chopped fresh coriander (cilantro) leaves

salt

freshly ground black pepper

1 To make the dressing, whisk the olive oil with the lime juice, vinegar, sugar, cumin and cayenne pepper in a large bowl. Stir in the garlic and coriander, then season with salt and freshly ground black pepper.

2 Add the corn, capsicum, tomatoes, celery and onion to the bowl, and toss with the dressing to combine. Serve garnished with the coriander sprigs.

Substitute the capsicum with canned red kidney beans – just rinse and drain before adding. If you like a stronger flavour, crumble goat's or sheep's cheese over the salad.

Per serving
*834 kJ, 199 kcal, 3 g protein, 14 g fat
(2 g saturated fat), 15 g carbohydrate
(6 g sugars), 4 g fibre, 306 mg sodium*

Mixed salad leaves with flowers and blueberries

PREPARATION 15 minutes
SERVES 4

1 small oakleaf lettuce, torn into bite-sized pieces

85 g (3 oz) rocket (arugula)

⅔ cup (100 g) blueberries

1⅓ cups (80 g) alfalfa sprouts

30 g (1 oz) mixed edible flowers, including some or all
of the following: nasturtiums, borage, violas or pansies,
and herb flowers such as sage and rosemary

Honey mustard dressing

¼ cup (60 ml) grapeseed oil

juice of 1 small lemon

1 teaspoon dijon mustard

1 teaspoon honey

salt

freshly ground black pepper

1 To make the dressing, whisk the oil with the lemon juice,
mustard and honey in a large shallow salad bowl. Season
with salt and freshly ground black pepper.

2 Add the lettuce and rocket to the bowl, and toss to coat
with the dressing. Sprinkle the salad with the blueberries.
Arrange the alfalfa and flowers on top and serve at once.

This pretty summer salad
is a colourful combination
of edible flowers, salad
leaves, alfalfa sprouts and
juicy fresh blueberries.
Some large supermarkets
sell packs of edible flowers,
or you can pick them from
your garden – choose those
that have not been sprayed
with pesticides.

Per serving
*655 kJ, 157 kcal, 2 g protein, 14 g fat
(1 g saturated fat), 6 g carbohydrate
(5 g sugars), 1 g fibre, 195 mg sodium*

Chicken and noodle salad

Use the meat from a barbecued or roasted chicken in this recipe.
Kecap manis is a thick, sweet Indonesian soy sauce. You'll find it
in larger supermarkets.

PREPARATION 20 minutes

COOKING 10 minutes

SERVES 2

100 g (3½ oz) dried rice vermicelli

1 Lebanese or other small cucumber

¾ cup (110 g) shredded cooked
chicken

½ carrot, cut into thin matchsticks

½ small red capsicum (bell pepper),
cut into thin matchsticks

2 spring onions (scallions), diagonally
sliced

6 fresh mint leaves, shredded

2 tablespoons roughly chopped fresh
coriander (cilantro) leaves

Lime and chilli dressing

2 teaspoons lime juice

2 teaspoons sweet chilli sauce

1 teaspoon kecap manis

1 teaspoon vegetable oil

1 Cook the noodles in a saucepan of boiling water according
to the packet instructions, until softened. Drain well.

2 While the noodles are cooking, cut the cucumber in half
lengthwise and scoop out the seeds. Cut the cucumber into
thin slices on the diagonal.

3 Combine the cucumber in a large bowl with the chicken,
carrot, capsicum, spring onions, mint, coriander and
drained noodles.

4 To make the dressing, whisk the lime juice, sweet chilli
sauce, kecap manis and oil in a small bowl.

5 Add the dressing to the salad and toss until well
combined. Serve immediately.

Use hokkien (egg) noodles instead
of rice noodles, and prepare them
according to the packet instructions.
Replace the chicken with thin strips
of cooked beef or pork.

Per serving
*1403 kJ, 335 kcal, 17 g protein, 7 g fat
(1 g saturated fat), 50 g carbohydrate
(6 g sugars), 3 g fibre, 343 mg sodium*

Chicken and raspberry salad with lime vinaigrette

If you are pressed for time, you can use smoked turkey or chicken breast instead of cooking the chicken. You can use slivered almonds instead of the pine nuts, and lemon juice in place of lime.

PREPARATION 15 minutes
COOKING 10 minutes
SERVES 4

¼ cup (40 g) pine nuts

1 green lettuce, such as butter (Boston) lettuce, leaves separated

⅔ cup (85 g) raspberries

1 tablespoon olive oil

2 boneless, skinless chicken breasts

salt

freshly ground black pepper

Lime vinaigrette

2 tablespoons lime juice

1 teaspoon raspberry vinegar

1 teaspoon grated lime zest

½ teaspoon sugar

pinch of salt

50 ml (1¾ fl oz) olive oil

1 Toast the pine nuts in a dry frying pan. Remove from the pan and set aside to cool.

2 Divide the lettuce among four serving plates and arrange the raspberries on top.

3 To make the vinaigrette, combine the lime juice with the vinegar, lime zest, sugar and salt. Whisk in the oil.

4 Heat the oil in a frying pan over medium heat. Season the chicken with salt and freshly ground black pepper. Sauté for 3–4 minutes on each side, until the chicken is cooked through. Remove from the pan and briefly cool, then cut crosswise into thin slices.

5 Divide the chicken slices among the salads. Drizzle the vinaigrette over each serving and lightly toss. Sprinkle with the pine nuts and serve immediately.

Per serving
1925 kJ, 460 kcal, 39 g protein, 33 g fat
(6 g saturated fat), 4 g carbohydrate
(3 g sugars), 2 g fibre, 407 mg sodium

Green pea salad
with chervil dressing

You can prepare the vegetables, ham, cheese and dressing in advance. Wait until just before serving to assemble the salads in the bowls and drizzle with the dressing.

PREPARATION 15 minutes
COOKING 5 minutes
SERVES 4

150 g (5 oz) snow peas (mangetout)

2 cups (300 g) frozen peas

125 g (4 oz) sliced ham, chopped

100 g (3½ oz) edam or gouda cheese, cut into cubes

Chervil dressing

¾ cup (200 g) natural (plain) yogurt

2 tablespoons lemon juice

1 teaspoon grated lemon zest

2 tablespoons finely chopped fresh chervil or parsley

pinch of salt

freshly ground black pepper

sugar, to taste

1 Add the snow peas and frozen peas to a large saucepan of boiling water. Bring back to a boil, then reduce the heat and simmer for 2 minutes. Drain all the peas in a colander, then rinse under cold water and drain well. Spread the peas on a thick layer of paper towel to dry.

2 To make the dressing, put the yogurt in a bowl and stir in the lemon juice, lemon zest and chervil or parsley. Season to taste with salt, freshly ground black pepper and sugar.

3 Arrange the peas with the ham and cheese in individual bowls or on individual plates. Drizzle with the dressing and serve immediately.

Use sugarsnap peas or baby green beans in addition to, or instead of, the snow peas and frozen peas.

Per serving
913 kJ, 218 kcal, 21 g protein, 11 g fat (6 g saturated fat), 9 g carbohydrate (5 g sugars), 5 g fibre, 839 mg sodium

Quick pasta and noodle salads

You can add a whole host of seasonal ingredients to pasta or noodles for a quick one-pot meal. For the best flavour, add a dressing to pasta while it's still hot, then serve warm, or prepare ahead to serve cold.

Italian summer salad

PREPARATION 10 minutes • **COOKING** 15 minutes • **SERVES** 4

Cook **250 g (8 oz) penne** in a large saucepan of salted boiling water according to the packet instructions. Drain, transfer to a large bowl and toss with a dressing made from **2 tablespoons extra virgin olive oil, 1 tablespoon lemon juice, ¼ cup (15 g) finely chopped fresh basil and 1 crushed clove garlic.** Season with **salt and freshly ground black pepper.** Halve **200 g (7 oz) red and yellow cherry tomatoes,** cube **150 g (5 oz) fresh mozzarella** and thinly slice **200 g (7 oz) roasted red capsicums (bell peppers)** from a jar. Add the vegetables and mozzarella to the pasta and toss to combine.

Per serving *1894 kJ, 453 kcal, 18 g protein, 22 g fat (7 g saturated fat), 46 g carbohydrate (2 g sugars), 4 g fibre, 495 mg sodium*

Chicken and sugarsnap noodle salad

PREPARATION 10 minutes • **COOKING** 15 minutes • **SERVES** 4

Steam **200 g (7 oz) sugarsnap peas** for 4 minutes. Drain, rinse under cold water, then drain again. Cook **200 g (7 oz) dried egg noodles** according to the packet instructions. Drain, transfer to a bowl and toss while hot with a dressing made from **2 tablespoons vegetable oil, 2 tablespoons lemon juice, 1 tablespoon tahini, 1 tablespoon soy sauce, 1 teaspoon toasted sesame oil, 1 crushed clove garlic and 2 teaspoons grated fresh ginger.** Cool for 15 minutes, then toss with the sugarsnap peas and **240 g (8 oz) cold cooked chicken strips.**

Per serving *1827 kJ, 437 kcal, 26 g protein, 19 g fat (3 g saturated fat), 38 g carbohydrate (2 g sugars), 3 g fibre, 248 mg sodium*

Italian summer salad

Easy pasta niçoise salad

PREPARATION 10 minutes • **COOKING** 15 minutes • **SERVES** 4

Cook **250 g (8 oz) pasta shapes,** such as conchiglie, in a saucepan of salted boiling water according to the packet instructions. Drain, transfer to a large bowl and toss with ¼ **cup (60 ml) French dressing** (page 13). Season with **salt and freshly ground black pepper.** Drain and flake a **200 g (7 oz) can tuna,** chop ¼ **cup (30 g) pitted black olives** and grate **1 large carrot.** Add to the pasta with **100 g (3½ oz) cooked green beans.** Top the salad with **1 quartered, hard-boiled egg.**

Per serving *1523 kJ, 364 kcal, 17 g protein, 13 g fat (2 g saturated fat), 45 g carbohydrate (1 g sugars), 3 g fibre, 405 mg sodium*

Capsicum and salami salad

PREPARATION 10 minutes • **COOKING** 15 minutes • **SERVES** 4

Cook **250 g (8 oz) pasta shapes,** such as fusilli, in a saucepan of salted boiling water according to the packet instructions. Drain, transfer to a large bowl and toss with ¼ **cup (60 ml) French dressing** (page 13). Season with **salt and freshly ground black pepper.** Thinly slice **1 red, 1 green and 1 yellow capsicum (bell pepper), 1 small red onion** and **100 g (3½ oz) salami.** Gently toss the vegetables and salami through the pasta with **100 g (3½ oz) rocket (arugula).**

Per serving *1755 kJ, 419 kcal, 14 g protein, 20 g fat (4 g saturated fat), 46 g carbohydrate (3 g sugars), 3 g fibre, 531 mg sodium*

Trout and cucumber salad

PREPARATION 10 minutes • **COOKING** 15 minutes • **SERVES** 4

Whisk ¼ **cup (60 ml) olive oil,** the **grated zest and juice of 1 small lemon** and ¼ **cup (7 g) chopped watercress** in a large bowl. Season with **salt and freshly ground black pepper.** Cook **250 g (8 oz) pasta shapes,** such as farfalle, in a saucepan of salted boiling water according to the packet instructions. Drain and toss with the dressing. Flake the flesh from **225 g (8 oz) cooked trout fillets** and dice ½ **small cucumber.** Toss with the pasta and **1 tablespoon drained capers.**

Per serving *1745 kJ, 417 kcal, 21 g protein, 17 g fat (3 g saturated fat), 44 g carbohydrate (<1 g sugars), 2 g fibre, 68 mg sodium*

Autumn

The cooler weather and shorter days invite heartier, more substantial salads, filled with mushrooms, earthy root vegetables, legumes, pulses and grains, flavoured with warming, fragrant spices and seasonings, and topped with soft, crumbly cheeses.

Pumpkin and lentil salad

Like most salads, this recipe is high in fibre, but the protein from the lentils, pistachios and cheese means that it is hearty and satisfying enough to be served on its own, or with bread, as a light main meal.

PREPARATION 15 minutes,
  plus cooling
COOKING 1 hour
SERVES 4

½ cup (100 g) puy or small blue-green
  lentils

½ cup (125 ml) salt-reduced vegetable
  or chicken stock

750 g (1½ lb) pumpkin (winter squash),
  cut into chunks

2 tablespoons olive oil

1 cup (35 g) rocket (arugula)

5 sprigs fresh mint, leaves picked

½ cup (75 g) raw pistachios

1 tablespoon extra virgin olive oil

juice of ½ lemon

2 teaspoons ground sumac

freshly ground black pepper

125 g (4 oz) soft goat's cheese

1 Combine the lentils, stock and ½ cup (125 ml) water in a large saucepan. Bring to a boil, then reduce the heat to low. Simmer, covered, for 1 hour, until the lentils are soft and all of the liquid has been absorbed. Allow to cool.

2 While the lentils are cooking, preheat the oven to 220°C (425°F/Gas 7). Toss the pumpkin chunks with the olive oil and arrange in a single layer on a baking tray. Bake for 25 minutes, until the pumpkin is soft and turning golden brown at the edges. Allow to cool.

3 Combine the lentils, pumpkin, rocket, mint and pistachios in a large bowl. Sprinkle with the extra virgin olive oil, lemon juice and sumac, and season with freshly ground black pepper. Using a large spoon, gently stir to combine the ingredients.

4 Serve the salad in the bowl or on a large platter, with the goat's cheese crumbled over the top.

To increase the fibre even further, leave the skin on the pumpkin. This method works best with thin-skinned varieties such as butternut pumpkin (squash).

Per serving
1843 kJ, 440 kcal, 19 g protein, 31 g fat
(8 g saturated fat), 24 g carbohydrate
(9 g sugars), 7 g fibre, 251 mg sodium

Chicken and sweet potato salad

This wholesome salad is a riot of flavours and textures. Slices of poached chicken, sweet potatoes and salad vegetables are served on a bed of leafy greens with a chunky pineapple salsa.

PREPARATION 30 minutes

COOKING 15 minutes

SERVES 4

1 kg (2 lb) orange sweet potatoes (kumara), scrubbed and sliced

4 boneless, skinless chicken breasts, about 150 g (5 oz) each

pinch of ground cinnamon

pinch of ground cumin

4 cups (200 g) mixed salad leaves

4 tomatoes, cut into thin wedges

¼ telegraph (long) cucumber, sliced

2 tablespoons chopped fresh coriander (cilantro)

2 tablespoons toasted sunflower seeds

2 spring onions (scallions), shredded

Pineapple salsa

½ ripe pineapple, about 350 g (12 oz), chopped

½ red capsicum (bell pepper), diced

½ small red onion, finely chopped

2 tablespoons chopped fresh mint

¼ teaspoon mild chilli powder

pinch of ground cinnamon

pinch of ground cumin

juice of ½ lime

Lime and soy dressing

juice of ½ lime

2 tablespoons vegetable oil

1 teaspoon caster (superfine) sugar

dash of soy sauce, or to taste

1 Cook the sweet potato slices in a saucepan of boiling water for 6–8 minutes, until just tender. Drain and leave to cool.

2 Poach the chicken in a frying pan of simmering water for 4–6 minutes, until cooked through. Drain and set aside to cool, then cut into slices.

3 Put the chicken and sweet potato slices in a large bowl and sprinkle with the cinnamon and cumin.

4 To make the salsa, put the pineapple, capsicum, onion, mint, chilli powder, cinnamon, cumin and lime juice in a bowl and gently toss to combine.

5 To make the dressing, whisk the lime juice, oil, sugar and soy sauce in a large shallow salad bowl.

6 Add the salad leaves to the bowl with the dressing and toss to coat. Arrange the chicken, sweet potato, tomatoes and cucumber on top of the leaves. Scatter the coriander, sunflower seeds and spring onions over the salad. Serve with the pineapple salsa on the side.

Per serving
*2334 kJ, 558 kcal, 42 g protein, 21 g fat
(4 g saturated fat), 50 g carbohydrate
(27 g sugars), 10 g fibre, 188 mg sodium*

Corn and whole-wheat salad

Grains of whole wheat have a distinctive sweet, nutty flavour. Here they are mixed with corn, toasted walnuts and crisp vegetables in a fragrant dressing to make a nutritious salad that is substantial enough to serve as a well-balanced main course.

PREPARATION 20 minutes,
  plus cooling
COOKING 25 minutes
SERVES 4

300 g (10 oz) pre-cooked whole-wheat
  grains (wheat berries)
1 bay leaf
2 corn cobs
2 teaspoons canola oil
⅔ cup (85 g) walnut pieces
1 red capsicum (bell pepper), chopped
1¼ cups (115 g) sliced button
  mushrooms
½ cucumber, cut into small chunks
1 tablespoon finely chopped fresh mint
salt
freshly ground black pepper
1 hard-boiled egg, to garnish
fresh mint sprigs, to garnish

Orange dressing
1 tablespoon walnut oil
1 tablespoon canola oil
1 tablespoon orange juice
½ teaspoon finely grated orange zest
1 teaspoon dijon mustard
salt
freshly ground black pepper

Per serving
*1999 kJ, 478 kcal, 14 g protein, 29 g fat
(2 g saturated fat), 43 g carbohydrate
(4 g sugars), 11 g fibre, 359 mg sodium*

1 Bring 3½ cups (875 ml) water to a boil in a saucepan. Add the whole-wheat grains and the bay leaf, and simmer for 15–20 minutes, until the whole wheat is tender and all the liquid has been absorbed. Discard the bay leaf and tip the whole-wheat grains into a bowl.

2 While the whole-wheat grains are cooking, preheat the grill (broiler) to medium–high. Brush the corn cobs all over with the canola oil, then put them on the grill rack. Grill (broil), turning frequently, for 10 minutes, until tender and lightly charred. Set aside.

3 Meanwhile, lightly toast the walnut pieces in a small dry frying pan over medium heat, stirring them frequently until fragrant. Set aside to cool.

4 When the corn is cool enough to handle, cut the kernels off the cobs with a sharp knife and add them to the bowl with the whole-wheat grains.

5 To make the dressing, whisk together the oils, orange juice, orange zest and mustard. Season with salt and freshly ground black pepper.

6 Drizzle the dressing over the warm whole-wheat grains and corn, and toss to coat. Set aside to cool completely.

7 Gently toss the red capsicum, mushrooms, cucumber, mint and toasted walnuts with the whole-wheat mixture. Taste and season with salt and freshly ground black pepper, if needed. Serve the salad at room temperature, garnished with slices of hard-boiled egg and some fresh mint sprigs.

Cos salad with chunky tomato vinaigrette

PREPARATION 15 minutes
SERVES 6

1 large cos (romaine) lettuce, torn into bite-sized pieces
¼ cup (35 g) crumbled fetta

Chunky tomato vinaigrette
2 large ripe tomatoes, halved, seeded and coarsely chopped
⅓ cup (10 g) loosely packed fresh basil
2 tablespoons tomato sauce (ketchup)
2 tablespoons olive oil
1 tablespoon balsamic vinegar
1 small clove garlic, crushed
½ teaspoon salt

1 To make the vinaigrette, combine the tomatoes, basil, tomato sauce, olive oil, balsamic vinegar, garlic and salt in a food processor. Chop in short bursts until the mixture is blended but still chunky.

2 Toss the lettuce with the vinaigrette in a large salad bowl. Sprinkle with the fetta and serve at once.

The chunky tomato vinaigrette also makes a flavoursome pasta sauce or topping for barbecued or grilled meats and chicken. It can be made several hours before needed and kept refrigerated.

Cheese is high in calcium and protein, and a good source of vitamin B$_{12}$.

Per serving
373 kJ, 89 kcal, 2 g protein, 8 g fat
(2 g saturated fat), 3 g carbohydrate
(3 g sugars), 1 g fibre, 336 mg sodium

Carrot and almond salad with raspberry vinaigrette

PREPARATION 15 minutes
COOKING 10 minutes
SERVES 4

500 g (1 lb) carrots, thinly sliced on the diagonal
¼ cup (30 g) slivered or sliced almonds
1 spring onion (scallion), thinly sliced

Raspberry vinaigrette
2 tablespoons raspberry vinegar
1 tablespoon olive oil
1 tablespoon honey
¼ teaspoon salt
¼ teaspoon freshly ground black pepper

1 To make the vinaigrette, whisk the vinegar, oil, honey, salt and freshly ground black pepper in a small bowl.

2 Steam the carrots over a saucepan of simmering water for about 8 minutes, until just tender. Rinse the carrots under cold running water, then drain.

3 Toss the carrots, almonds, spring onion and vinaigrette in a serving bowl until combined. Serve at once.

Almonds, like most nuts, are a rich source of vitamins, especially folate and vitamin E. There are two varieties of almond. The edible variety is sweet while the inedible, or bitter, almond contains a form of cyanide.

Per serving
599 kJ, 143 kcal, 3 g protein, 9 g fat
(<1 g saturated fat), 13 g carbohydrate
(13 g sugars), 4 g fibre, 210 mg sodium

Quinoa and chickpea salad

One of the first grains to be dubbed a 'superfood', quinoa is a complete protein (possessing all nine essential amino acids) and is packed full of nutrients that may help regulate blood pressure.

PREPARATION 15 minutes

COOKING 15 minutes

SERVES 4

1⅓ cups (270 g) quinoa

2 cups (500 ml) salt-reduced chicken stock

400 g (14 oz) can chickpeas, rinsed and drained

1 cup (140 g) finely chopped celery

1 cup (155 g) finely chopped red capsicum (bell pepper)

⅓ cup (50 g) finely chopped red onion

finely chopped fresh coriander (cilantro) leaves, to garnish

Honey and lime vinaigrette

juice of 1 large lime

2 tablespoons extra virgin olive oil

2 teaspoons honey

⅛ teaspoon chilli powder

1 tablespoon chopped fresh coriander (cilantro)

1 Rinse the quinoa under cold running water until the water runs clear. Bring the stock to a boil in a saucepan over high heat. Stir in the quinoa and reduce the heat to medium–low. Cover and simmer the quinoa for 10–12 minutes, until most of the liquid has been absorbed. Turn off the heat and set aside, covered, for 5 minutes. Fluff the grains with a fork and leave to cool.

2 Meanwhile, to make the vinaigrette, put the lime juice in a small bowl and gradually whisk in the oil in a steady stream. Whisk in the honey, chilli powder and coriander.

3 Combine the chickpeas, celery, capsicum and onion in a bowl. Add the quinoa and toss to combine.

4 Pour the vinaigrette over the salad and toss to coat. Serve sprinkled with the chopped coriander.

> Rinsing the quinoa before cooking removes the grain's saponin, which can sometimes make it taste bitter.

Per serving
1824 kJ, 436 kcal, 15 g protein, 15 g fat (2 g saturated fat), 63 g carbohydrate (8 g sugars), 8 g fibre, 504 mg sodium

Escalivada

'Escalivada' comes from a Catalan word meaning 'to roast over embers'. It is traditionally served as a first course or a side dish with barbecued or roasted meats. This oven-roasted version is a quick, easy alternative if you don't have a charcoal grill.

PREPARATION 10 minutes
COOKING 1 hour
SERVES 4–6

1 red capsicum (bell pepper)

1 yellow capsicum (bell pepper)

2 ripe tomatoes

2 red onions

1 eggplant (aubergine), about 400 g (14 oz)

4 baby leeks or thick spring onions (scallions), fleshy white part only

1 tablespoon chopped fresh thyme

Garlic dressing
1 head garlic

¼ cup (60 ml) extra virgin olive oil

salt

freshly ground black pepper

1 Preheat the oven to 180°C (350°F/Gas 4). Put the whole red and yellow capsicums, tomatoes, onions, eggplant and the head of garlic (from the garlic dressing) on a baking tray. Do not peel, core or cut any of the vegetables. Roast the vegetables for 40 minutes.

2 Add the leeks or spring onions to the tray and bake for a further 20 minutes, until all the vegetables are very soft and slightly blackened. Remove from the oven.

3 When the vegetables are cool enough to handle, peel the capsicums, removing the seeds, and cut into long strips. Peel and seed the tomatoes, and cut into wedges. Peel the onions and cut into wedges. Scoop the eggplant flesh out of the skin with a large spoon, and cut the flesh into long strips. Peel the outer layer from the leeks or spring onions. Reserve any juices from the tray. Arrange the vegetables on a serving platter.

4 To make the dressing, use a sharp serrated knife to cut the garlic head crosswise at the widest point. Squeeze the garlic flesh into a small bowl, add the olive oil and some of the reserved vegetable juices, as desired, and season with salt and freshly ground black pepper.

5 Drizzle the dressing over the roasted vegetables, sprinkle with the thyme and serve warm.

Per serving
828 kJ, 198 kcal, 5 g protein, 15 g fat (2 g saturated fat), 12 g carbohydrate (10 g sugars), 8 g fibre, 177 mg sodium

Mushroom salad with quail eggs

Full-flavoured shiitake mushrooms are poached with more delicate chanterelles and oyster mushrooms, then tossed with herbs and topped with softly poached quail eggs.

PREPARATION 20 minutes

COOKING 25 minutes

SERVES 4

2 French shallots, thinly sliced

1 clove garlic, crushed

1 teaspoon coriander seeds, crushed

1 bay leaf

200 ml (7 fl oz) vegetable stock

125 g (4 oz) shiitake mushrooms

125 g (4 oz) oyster mushrooms

125 g (4 oz) chanterelles

2 tablespoons dry Marsala or medium sherry

150 g (5 oz) baby leeks, or 1 medium leek, white part only, sliced

1 tablespoon truffle or walnut oil

1 teaspoon lemon juice

freshly ground black pepper

12 quail eggs

1 oakleaf lettuce, leaves separated

85 g (3 oz) mixed fresh herbs, such as rocket (arugula), sorrel and flat-leaf parsley

1 Put the shallots, garlic, crushed coriander seeds and bay leaf in a large saucepan. Add the stock and bring to a boil, then cover and simmer for 10 minutes.

2 Meanwhile, thickly slice the shiitake mushrooms. Break the oyster mushrooms and the chanterelles into smaller pieces (leave small ones whole).

3 Add the Marsala or sherry and the shiitake mushrooms to the hot stock. Gently simmer for 3 minutes, then add the chanterelles and oyster mushrooms, and cook for 1–2 minutes. Remove the mushrooms using a slotted spoon and transfer to a bowl.

4 Add the sliced leeks to the simmering stock and cook for 3–4 minutes, until tender. Remove with a slotted spoon and add to the mushrooms.

5 Rapidly boil the stock for about 5 minutes, until syrupy and reduced to about 100 ml (3½ fl oz). Strain the liquid through a very fine sieve into a small bowl. Whisk in the oil and lemon juice, and season with some freshly ground black pepper. Pour ¼ cup (60 ml) of this dressing over the mushrooms and leeks, and gently toss. Leave to cool.

6 Cook the eggs in boiling water for 1–2 minutes, depending on whether you prefer them soft or medium boiled. Plunge into cold water to cool, then peel.

7 Put the lettuce leaves and herbs in a mixing bowl. Drizzle with the remaining dressing and toss to coat. Arrange the salad leaves on one side of four plates and the mushroom mixture on the other side. Cut the eggs in half and divide among the plates. Serve at once.

Per serving
652 kJ, 156 kcal, 8 g protein, 8 g fat
(1 g saturated fat), 10 g carbohydrate
(7 g sugars), 5 g fibre, 336 mg sodium

Quinoa and cranberry salad

Always rinse quinoa well before use, to remove the bitter-tasting saponin layer from the surface of the grains. You can replace the quinoa or brown rice with couscous in this side salad, and add some chopped fresh mint.

PREPARATION 10 minutes
COOKING 25–40 minutes
SERVES 4

1½ cups (300 g) quinoa, rinsed and drained, or brown rice

½ cup (60 g) dried cranberries

½ cup (70 g) mixed seeds, such as pepitas (pumpkin seeds) and sunflower seeds

400 g (14 oz) can mixed beans, rinsed and drained

½ cup (15 g) roughly chopped fresh flat-leaf parsley

Dressing

1½ tablespoons balsamic vinegar

2 tablespoons extra virgin olive oil

freshly ground black pepper

1 Put the quinoa or brown rice in a small saucepan with 3 cups (750 ml) water and bring to a boil over high heat. Reduce the heat to low, then cover and simmer until all the water has been absorbed, about 15 minutes for the quinoa or 30 minutes for brown rice.

2 Meanwhile, put the cranberries in a small heatproof bowl, cover with boiling water and soak for 10 minutes.

3 Put the mixed seeds in a dry frying pan over medium heat and cook, stirring occasionally, for 3–4 minutes, until they start to brown. Tip the seeds into a salad bowl.

4 Drain the cranberries and add to the salad bowl with the mixed beans, parsley and quinoa or rice, and mix well.

5 To make the dressing, whisk the vinegar and oil in a small bowl, and season with freshly ground black pepper.

6 Stir the dressing through the salad. Serve immediately or refrigerate until required.

Quinoa is a high-protein grain that originated in South America. The Incas recognised its nutritional value, calling it 'the mother of all grains'. White, red and black quinoa are available, so use a mixture for added colour.

Per serving
1942 kJ, 464 kcal, 17 g protein, 13 g fat (2 g saturated fat), 71 g carbohydrate (5 g sugars), 13 g fibre, 289 mg sodium

Baby leek salad with tarragon

Here, young tender leeks are marinated in a piquant tarragon vinaigrette and then sprinkled with hard-boiled eggs and toasted breadcrumbs.

PREPARATION 10 minutes
COOKING 15 minutes
SERVES 4

¼ cup (20 g) fresh coarse wholegrain or white breadcrumbs

2 eggs

500 g (1 lb) baby leeks, halved lengthwise

Tarragon vinaigrette

¼ cup (60 ml) peanut (groundnut) oil

2 teaspoons white wine vinegar

1 teaspoon dijon mustard

1 teaspoon chopped fresh tarragon

salt

freshly ground black pepper

1 Preheat the grill (broiler) to high. Line the grill pan or a baking tray with foil. Spread the breadcrumbs on the tray, then toast for 4 minutes, until golden and crunchy.

2 Bring a saucepan of water to a boil. Add the eggs and cook for 10 minutes. While the eggs are cooking, steam the leeks for 5–8 minutes, until just tender. (The leeks can be steamed over the eggs.)

3 Meanwhile, to make the vinaigrette, whisk the peanut oil, vinegar, mustard and tarragon in a bowl, and season with salt and freshly ground black pepper.

4 Drain the eggs and cool under cold running water, then peel and finely chop them.

5 Arrange the leeks on a platter or individual serving plates and drizzle with the vinaigrette. Leave to cool, then scatter over the eggs and toasted breadcrumbs. Serve before the crumbs lose their texture.

This makes an excellent side salad or starter, or a light lunch for two with crusty bread. For the best flavour, serve the salad at cool room temperature, not chilled.

Per serving
886 kJ, 212 kcal, 7 g protein, 17 g fat (3 g saturated fat), 8 g carbohydrate (5 g sugars), 4 g fibre, 265 mg sodium

Noodle and omelette salad

Tasty Asian flavours mingle in this layered salad. Crisp vegetables and water chestnuts are topped with Chinese egg noodles, broccoli and bean sprouts, and thin strips of savoury omelette are the finishing touch.

PREPARATION 25 minutes
COOKING 10 minutes
SERVES 4

250 g (8 oz) broccoli, broken into florets

250 g (8 oz) hokkien (egg) noodles

2¾ cups (245 g) bean sprouts, trimmed

250 g (8 oz) baby bok choy, shredded

6 eggs

1 tablespoon milk or water

1 teaspoon soy sauce

2 teaspoons sunflower or vegetable oil

230 g (8 oz) can water chestnuts, drained and sliced or quartered

1 carrot, coarsely grated

1 red capsicum (bell pepper), thinly sliced

5 spring onions (scallions), thinly sliced

¼ cup (15 g) coarsely chopped fresh coriander (cilantro)

¼ cup (40 g) sesame seeds

Rice vinegar dressing

2 teaspoons caster (superfine) sugar

¼ cup (60 ml) rice vinegar

1½ tablespoons soy sauce

2 tablespoons sesame oil

1 tablespoon grated fresh ginger

salt

freshly ground black pepper

Per serving
1881 kJ, 449 kcal, 21 g protein, 26 g fat
(5 g saturated fat), 29 g carbohydrate
(10 g sugars), 8 g fibre, 958 mg sodium

1 Drop the broccoli into a large saucepan of boiling water and cook for 10 seconds. Add the noodles, breaking them up as you drop them into the water, then remove the pan from the heat. Add the bean sprouts and leave to soak for 4 minutes.

2 Add the bok choy to the pan of hot water and stir until slightly wilted, then drain the noodles and vegetables well. Transfer to a mixing bowl.

3 Lightly beat the eggs with the milk or water and the soy sauce. Heat ½ teaspoon of the sunflower or vegetable oil in a non-stick omelette pan. Add one-quarter of the egg mixture. Cook for 2 minutes, gently stirring and lifting the edges of the omelette to let the uncooked egg mixture run onto the pan, until the omelette is set. Slide onto a plate. Repeat to make another three omelettes, removing and stacking them as they cook. When all the omelettes are cooked, cut them into thin strips.

4 To make the dressing, whisk the sugar, vinegar, soy sauce, sesame oil and ginger in a large bowl, and season with salt and freshly ground black pepper.

5 Drizzle half the dressing over the noodle mixture and toss to coat. Add the water chestnuts, carrot and capsicum to the bowl with the remaining dressing and toss to coat.

6 Arrange the carrot mixture on a large platter and spoon the noodle mixture on top. Sprinkle with the spring onions, coriander and sesame seeds, then add the omelette strips and serve immediately.

Indian-style rice salad with chicken

The rice, with its slightly chewy texture and Indian spices, provides the perfect backdrop for tender chicken, crunchy raw vegetables, sweet grapes and toasted nuts.

PREPARATION 50 minutes,
  plus cooling
COOKING 30 minutes
SERVES 6

1 tablespoon sunflower or vegetable oil

1½ cups (300 g) basmati rice, rinsed

1 onion, finely chopped

1 teaspoon grated fresh ginger

¼ teaspoon garam masala

¼ teaspoon ground coriander

½ teaspoon curry powder

3 cups (750 ml) hot chicken or
  vegetable stock, or water

1 bay leaf

3 large stalks celery, chopped

4 spring onions (scallions), chopped

1 large carrot, grated

150 g (5 oz) seedless red grapes,
  halved

500 g (1 lb) chopped cooked chicken

¼ cup (7 g) chopped fresh flat-leaf
  parsley

oakleaf or other soft lettuce leaves

¾ cup (75 g) toasted pecans, roughly
  chopped, or toasted flaked almonds

Citrus dressing

⅓ cup (80 ml) orange juice

2 teaspoons lime juice

1 tablespoon sunflower or vegetable oil

1 tablespoon snipped fresh chives

salt

freshly ground black pepper

1 Heat the oil in a large saucepan over medium heat. Add the rice and stir until thoroughly coated. Cook, stirring frequently, for 1 minute. Add the onion, ginger, garam masala, coriander and curry powder, and cook, stirring, for 3–4 minutes, until the onion starts to soften.

2 Add the stock or water and bay leaf to the rice mixture, and bring to a boil. Reduce the heat, cover and simmer for 25 minutes, until the rice is tender. Discard the bay leaf and transfer the rice to a large bowl to cool.

3 Meanwhile, to make the dressing, whisk the orange juice, lime juice, oil and chives in a small bowl. Season with salt and freshly ground black pepper.

4 Add the celery, spring onions and carrot to the cooled rice. Reserve half the grapes and add the remainder to the rice along with the chicken and the parsley. Drizzle with the dressing and gently stir to combine.

5 Arrange a bed of lettuce leaves on each of six plates and pile the rice salad on top. Scatter the pecans or almonds and the remaining grapes over the top and serve.

Per serving
*2123 kJ, 507 kcal, 30 g protein, 20 g fat
(3 g saturated fat), 52 g carbohydrate
(10 g sugars), 4 g fibre, 895 mg sodium*

Vegetable risoni salad

Risoni is a fine, rice-shaped pasta that is perfect for salads. You can use any small pasta shapes in this recipe. Instead of baking the tomatoes, toss some chopped sun-dried or semi-dried tomatoes through the pasta.

PREPARATION 10 minutes
COOKING 15 minutes
SERVES 4

250 g (8 oz) red cherry tomatoes, halved

salt

freshly ground black pepper

375 g (13 oz) risoni

400 g (14 oz) broccoli, cut into florets

350 g (12 oz) thin asparagus spears, cut into thirds

250 g (8 oz) jar goat's cheese marinated in oil and herbs

1 Preheat the oven to 220°C (425°F/Gas 7). Line a baking tray with baking (parchment) paper. Place the tomatoes on the tray and season with salt and freshly ground black pepper. Bake for 10–15 minutes, until the tomatoes are heated through and slightly shrivelled.

2 Meanwhile, add the risoni to a large saucepan of salted boiling water and cook for 6 minutes, or according to the packet instructions, until al dente. Add the broccoli and asparagus for the last 2 minutes and cook until just tender. Drain the risoni and vegetables, and transfer to a large salad bowl.

3 Crumble the goat's cheese over the salad, drizzle with some of the oil from the jar and toss to combine. Top the salad with the tomatoes and serve immediately.

Instead of goat's cheese, use fetta, parmesan or blue cheese. Use other vegetables, such as broad (fava) beans, peas, or sliced yellow or green beans. Toss some sour cream or yogurt through the pasta.

Per serving
2454 kJ, 586 kcal, 31 g protein, 20 g fat (13 g saturated fat), 69 g carbohydrate (4 g sugars), 9 g fibre, 355 mg sodium

Potato and tuna salad

PREPARATION 15 minutes, plus 30 minutes chilling
COOKING 20 minutes
SERVES 4

6 small red-skinned or boiling (waxy) potatoes
1²/₃ cups (250 g) frozen peas
425 g (15 oz) can tuna in olive oil
2 carrots, grated
juice of 1 lemon
salt
freshly ground black pepper
1¼ cups (310 g) mayonnaise
4 hard-boiled eggs, quartered
snipped fresh chives or chopped flat-leaf parsley, to serve

1 Peel the potatoes or leave the skin on. Add the whole potatoes to a saucepan of boiling water and cook for 15 minutes, until just tender. Remove with a slotted spoon and drain. Add the peas to the boiling water and cook for 3 minutes, then drain and rinse under cold running water.

2 Slice the potatoes and place in a serving bowl. Drain the oil from the tuna into a bowl, then flake the tuna over the potatoes. Add the carrots and peas.

3 Add the lemon juice to the tuna oil. Season with salt and freshly ground black pepper, then add enough mayonnaise to make 350 ml (12 fl oz). Whisk until combined, then stir the dressing through the salad.

4 Arrange the eggs on top of the salad and sprinkle with the chives or parsley. Cover and chill for 30 minutes before serving.

Per serving
*3277 kJ (783 kcal), 36 g protein, 55 g fat
(8 g saturated fat), 36 g carbohydrate
(15 g sugars), 6 g fibre, 1304 mg sodium*

Chives are best chopped with a pair of scissors to avoid squashing and bruising the tender stalks.

Gado gado

PREPARATION 10 minutes
COOKING 15 minutes
SERVES 2

2 small carrots, diagonally sliced

85 g (3 oz) green beans, trimmed

125 g (4 oz) Chinese cabbage, cut into wedges

2 small boiling (waxy) potatoes, such as desiree,
  scrubbed and cut into quarters

50 g (1¾ oz) bean sprouts, trimmed

2 hard-boiled eggs, quartered

½ cup (125 g) ready-made satay sauce

Bring a saucepan of water to a boil over high heat.
  Add the carrots and cook for 4 minutes, until just tender.
  Using a slotted spoon, remove the carrots and refresh
  under cold water.

1 Blanch the beans and Chinese cabbage in the boiling
  water for 2 minutes, then remove with a slotted spoon and
  refresh under cold running water or in a bowl of
  cold water. Add the potatoes to the boiling water. Cook
  for 8 minutes, until tender, then drain.

2 Arrange the vegetables, bean sprouts and eggs on a
  serving plate. Serve drizzled with the satay sauce.

If you wish to make your
own satay sauce, use the
Peanut butter dressing
from page 63.

Per serving
*1538 kJ, 367 kcal, 15 g protein, 20 g fat
(6 g saturated fat), 32 g carbohydrate
(14 g sugars), 7 g fibre, 511 mg sodium*

Tuna, chickpea and dill salad

This high-protein, substantial salad is also high in beneficial fats from the tuna and the olive oil, as well as providing good amounts of fibre and anti-oxidants.

PREPARATION 20 minutes
SERVES 4

425 g (15 oz) can tuna in springwater, well drained, flaked

400 g (14 oz) can chickpeas, rinsed and drained

4 gherkins (pickles), finely chopped

4 radishes, thinly sliced

1 large stalk celery, thinly sliced

1 tablespoon baby capers, rinsed and squeezed dry

1 tablespoon chopped fresh dill

2 large hard-boiled eggs, quartered

2 tablespoons fresh chervil or small flat-leaf parsley leaves

Orange mustard dressing

1½ tablespoons extra virgin olive oil

2 tablespoons orange juice

1 tablespoon red wine vinegar

1 teaspoon dijon mustard

freshly ground black pepper

1 To make the dressing, put the oil, orange juice, vinegar and mustard in a small bowl. Season with freshly ground black pepper and whisk well to combine.

2 Put the tuna, chickpeas, gherkins, radishes, celery, capers and dill in a large salad bowl. Pour the dressing over the salad and gently toss to combine.

3 Arrange the egg quarters over the salad, sprinkle with the chervil or parsley and serve.

The salad can be prepared up to 3 hours in advance, but it is best to toss it with the dressing close to serving time.

Per serving
1516 kJ, 362 kcal, 29 g protein, 23 g fat (4 g saturated fat), 10 g carbohydrate (2 g sugars), 3 g fibre, 704 mg sodium

Bean and rice salad

Brown rice, with its outer bran layer intact, has three times the fibre of white rice and much higher levels of minerals and B-group vitamins. It does take longer to cook, but it is worth the effort for its nutty flavour and its superior nutritional value.

PREPARATION 30 minutes,
 plus overnight soaking
COOKING 1 hour 30 minutes
SERVES 4

¾ cup (150 g) black-eyed peas

1⅓ cups (260 g) long-grain brown rice

2 carrots, thinly sliced

125 g (4 oz) green beans, cut into short lengths

420 g (15 oz) can red kidney beans, rinsed and drained

400 g (14 oz) can chickpeas, rinsed and drained

1 large tomato, chopped

1 small red capsicum (bell pepper), chopped

1 small red onion, chopped

Mustard and thyme dressing

¼ cup (60 ml) red wine vinegar, or to taste

1 tablespoon canola oil

1 tablespoon wholegrain mustard

1 tablespoon chopped fresh thyme

1 clove garlic, crushed

freshly ground black pepper

1 Soak the black-eyed peas overnight in cold water. Drain and rinse under cold water. Place in a saucepan and cover with cold water. Bring to a boil, then reduce the heat to low and simmer for 45–60 minutes, until tender. Rinse well, drain, then set aside.

2 Put the rice in a saucepan, cover with water and bring to a boil. Reduce the heat to low and simmer for 30 minutes, or according to the packet instructions, until tender. Drain and set aside to cool.

3 Meanwhile, blanch the carrots in a saucepan of boiling water for 3 minutes. Add the green beans and blanch for a further 4 minutes, until the vegetables are tender. Drain and refresh under cold water, then drain.

4 Place the carrots and green beans in a large bowl and add the black-eyed peas, kidney beans, chickpeas, tomato, capsicum and onion.

5 To make the dressing, whisk the vinegar, oil, mustard, thyme and garlic in a small bowl. Season with freshly ground black pepper.

6 Drizzle the dressing over the salad and toss well to combine. Gently fold the rice into the salad and serve.

Per serving
2330 kJ, 557 kcal, 24 g protein, 9 g fat (<1 g saturated fat), 95 g carbohydrate (9 g sugars), 16 g fibre, 378 mg sodium

Chinese cabbage and peanut salad with ginger dressing

This crisp, Asian-style salad is an ideal side dish to serve with roast chicken and rice. Add the dressing just before serving to prevent the cabbage from wilting.

PREPARATION 20 minutes
SERVES 4

½ small Chinese cabbage

2 red capsicums (bell peppers), cut into thin strips

1 cucumber, seeded and thinly sliced

⅓ cup (50 g) roasted salted peanuts (groundnuts), coarsely chopped

1 small handful fresh coriander (cilantro) sprigs

Soy and ginger dressing

2 tablespoons sunflower or vegetable oil

1 teaspoon toasted sesame oil

1½ tablespoons white wine vinegar

1½ tablespoons soy sauce

1 small clove garlic, crushed

1 teaspoon grated fresh ginger

1–2 teaspoons honey

1 Halve the cabbage lengthwise and remove the stalk. Wash the halves and shake off the excess water, then slice the cabbage crosswise into thin strips. Place in a large salad bowl.

2 Add the capsicums and cucumber to the cabbage and toss to combine. Sprinkle the peanuts over the salad.

3 To make the dressing, whisk the oils, vinegar and soy sauce in a small bowl. Stir in the garlic and ginger, then add the honey, to taste.

4 Add the dressing to the salad and toss to combine. Stir the coriander sprigs through the salad and serve.

Per serving
796 kJ, 190 kcal, 5 g protein, 16 g fat (2 g saturated fat), 6 g carbohydrate (5 g sugars), 2 g fibre, 580 mg sodium

Fig and prosciutto salad

A simple salad of fresh figs and prosciutto makes a lovely first course. If fresh figs are not available, you can substitute dried figs – coarsely chop one soft, dried fig per person and sprinkle over the salad.

PREPARATION 15 minutes
SERVES 4

1 large oakleaf lettuce, leaves
   separated
4 ripe figs
100 g (3½ oz) prosciutto, cut into strips
16 fresh basil leaves, thinly sliced
40 g (1½ oz) parmesan

Orange vinaigrette
1½ tablespoons orange juice
1 teaspoon balsamic vinegar
1 teaspoon wholegrain mustard
½ teaspoon grated orange zest
⅓ cup (80 ml) olive oil

1 To make the vinaigrette, mix the orange juice, vinegar, mustard and orange zest in a small bowl. Whisk in the oil until thoroughly combined.

2 Place the lettuce in a large bowl. Drizzle the vinaigrette over the lettuce and gently mix to coat. Divide the lettuce among four serving plates.

3 Quarter the figs lengthwise. If desired, use a sharp knife to make small incisions just underneath the skin to make it easier to remove the flesh when eating.

4 Place the figs beside the lettuce. Arrange the prosciutto strips and basil over the figs and shave the parmesan over the top to serve.

This autumn salad goes perfectly with buttered hazelnut or walnut bread, or other dense breads.

Per serving
1252 kJ, 299 kcal, 12 g protein, 26 g fat
(7 g saturated fat), 6 g carbohydrate
(5 g sugars), 2 g fibre, 474 mg sodium

Chicken satay salad

Marinated chicken strips are threaded onto skewers, then cooked and served on top of a rice and crunchy vegetable mixture and drizzled with spicy peanut dressing. The chicken can be served on or off the skewers.

PREPARATION 30 minutes,
  plus 3 hours marinating
COOKING 20 minutes
SERVES 4

2 tablespoons vegetable oil

¼ cup (60 ml) soy sauce

1 tablespoon fish sauce

2 cloves garlic, crushed

2.5 cm (1 inch) piece fresh ginger,
  peeled and finely chopped

500 g (1 lb) boneless, skinless chicken
  breasts, cut into thin strips

1¼ cups (250 g) basmati rice, rinsed

100 g (3½ oz) snow peas (mangetout),
  halved

grated zest and juice of 2 limes

2 tablespoons chopped fresh coriander
  (cilantro)

½ small Chinese cabbage, shredded

¼ telegraph (long) cucumber, diced

4 spring onions (scallions), shredded

Spicy peanut dressing

1 small onion, finely chopped

¼ cup (60 g) crunchy peanut butter

1 red chilli, seeded and finely chopped

100 ml (3½ fl oz) light coconut milk

1 teaspoon caster (superfine) sugar

Per serving
2735 kJ, 653 kcal, 39 g protein, 28 g fat
(8 g saturated fat), 62 g carbohydrate
(7 g sugars),4 g fibre, 1196 mg sodium

1 Combine half the oil, 2 tablespoons of the soy sauce, the fish sauce, garlic and ginger in a bowl. Add the chicken and toss to coat. Cover and refrigerate for at least 3 hours.

2 Add the rice to a saucepan of boiling water and cook for 10 minutes, until almost tender. Add the snow peas for the last 2 minutes. Drain in a sieve and rinse with cold water.

3 Combine the lime zest and juice with the remaining oil and soy sauce in a large bowl. Add the rice and snow peas, coriander, Chinese cabbage, cucumber and spring onions, and toss together.

4 Preheat the grill (broiler). Lift the chicken strips out of the marinade, reserving the marinade, and thread onto metal skewers (or onto soaked bamboo skewers if you want to leave the chicken on them for serving). Grill (broil) for 8–10 minutes, turning to brown the chicken evenly, until cooked through.

5 Meanwhile, to make the dressing, put the onion, peanut butter, chilli, coconut milk, sugar and reserved marinade in a small saucepan. Bring to a boil, then reduce the heat and gently cook, stirring, for 5 minutes. If the dressing is too thick, add 2–3 tablespoons water.

6 Spread the salad over a large platter. Remove the chicken from the skewers and arrange on top of the salad. Drizzle the chicken with the dressing and serve warm or at cool room temperature.

Chicken caesar salad

A variation on the classic caesar salad, this one is more substantial as it includes chunks of tender chicken, green beans and tasty anchovy croutons, all tossed in a creamy yogurt dressing.

PREPARATION 10 minutes

COOKING 20 minutes

SERVES 4

200 g (7 oz) thin green beans

1–2 cos (romaine) lettuces, about 500 g (1 lb) in total, torn into bite-sized pieces

1 small head witlof (Belgian endive), sliced crosswise

4 stalks celery, sliced

400 g (14 oz) cooked boneless, skinless chicken breasts, cut into chunks

50 g (1¾ oz) can anchovy fillets

1 clove garlic, crushed

12 thin slices of baguette, about 100 g (3½ oz) in total

30 g (1 oz) parmesan, shaved

Caesar dressing

1 egg

¼ cup (60 ml) extra virgin olive oil

2 tablespoons low-fat natural (plain) yogurt

2 teaspoons sherry vinegar or wine vinegar

1 teaspoon dijon mustard

½ teaspoon worcestershire sauce

large pinch of caster (superfine) sugar

freshly ground black pepper

Per serving
2080 kJ, 497 kcal, 42 g protein, 28 g fat (7 g saturated fat), 19 g carbohydrate (6 g sugars), 6 g fibre, 1147 mg sodium

1 Preheat the oven to 200°C (400°F/Gas 6).

2 Add the beans to a saucepan of boiling water and cook for 3 minutes, until just tender. Drain and refresh under cold running water. Halve the beans and put into a large salad bowl. Add the lettuce, witlof, celery and chicken. Cover and refrigerate until serving time.

3 Tip the anchovies into a bowl with the oil from the can (about 1 tablespoon). Add the garlic and use a fork to mash it to a paste. Thinly spread the paste over one side of each slice of baguette. Arrange on a baking tray and bake for about 10 minutes, until the croutons are crisp and golden. Cool slightly, then break into pieces.

4 While the croutons are cooking, make the dressing. Put the egg in a saucepan, cover with cold water and bring to a boil. Reduce the heat and simmer for 10 minutes. Drain the egg and cool under cold running water, then peel and chop. Whisk the oil, yogurt, vinegar, mustard, worcestershire sauce and sugar in a bowl. Season with freshly ground black pepper, then stir in the egg.

5 Drizzle half of the dressing over the salad and toss until the ingredients are evenly coated. Add the croutons and toss again. Drizzle with the remaining dressing and then scatter with the parmesan shavings. Serve at once.

Warm potato and artichoke salad

This salad is a perfect partner for lamb or chicken, or can
be served as a starter before a light main course. The globe
artichoke is an edible thistle native to the Mediterranean
region and the tender heart is a classic antipasto vegetable.

PREPARATION 10 minutes

COOKING 25 minutes

SERVES 4

750 g (1½ lb) small new potatoes

400 g (14 oz) jar or can artichoke
   hearts, rinsed and drained

2 tablespoons olive oil

2 slices lean bacon, rind removed,
   finely chopped

1 red onion, halved and thinly sliced

1 red or yellow capsicum (bell pepper),
   cut into thin strips

75 g (2½ oz) rocket (arugula)

1 tablespoon balsamic vinegar

1 tablespoon dry white wine

salt

freshly ground black pepper

2 tablespoons toasted pine nuts

1 Add the potatoes to a saucepan of boiling water and cook
   for 15 minutes, until just tender. Drain well, then cut the
   potatoes in half, or into quarters if they are large.

2 While the potatoes are cooking, cut the artichoke hearts
   in half lengthwise and pat dry with paper towel. Heat half
   the oil in a non-stick frying pan over medium–high heat.
   Place the artichoke hearts in the pan in a single layer, cut
   side down, and cook for 2–3 minutes, until golden brown
   underneath. Turn and cook for 1 minute, until browned
   on the other side. Transfer the artichokes to a serving
   bowl. Add the potatoes and keep warm.

3 Heat the remaining oil in the frying pan. Sauté the bacon
   and onion over medium–high heat for 1–2 minutes, then
   add the capsicum and cook for a further 1 minute. Using
   a slotted spoon, transfer the bacon, onion and capsicum
   to the bowl with the potatoes and artichokes. Scatter the
   rocket on top.

4 Return the pan to the heat and add the balsamic vinegar
   and wine. Tilt the pan to swirl and mix the vinegar and
   wine with the cooking juices. Pour over the salad, season
   with salt and freshly ground black pepper, then gently
   toss until well combined. Sprinkle the toasted pine nuts
   over the salad and serve.

Per serving
*1353 kJ, 323 kcal, 12 g protein, 17 g fat
(2 g saturated fat), 29 g carbohydrate
(5 g sugars), 7 g fibre, 660 mg sodium*

Bean salad with tuna

Serve this bean salad with toasted crusty bread rubbed with garlic. The salad also makes a very good filling for sandwich rolls or pita pockets.

PREPARATION 20 minutes

SERVES 4

400 g (14 oz) can cannellini beans, rinsed and drained

2 x 185 g (6 oz) cans tuna in oil, drained

2 tomatoes, chopped

⅓ cup (60 g) pitted green olives, coarsely chopped

1 tablespoon capers, rinsed and squeezed dry, coarsely chopped

1 teaspoon dried oregano

Dressing

100 g (3½ oz) mayonnaise

1½ tablespoons ajvar

1½ tablespoons white balsamic vinegar

1 Put the cannellini beans in a large salad bowl. Break up the tuna a little with a fork and add it to the beans.

2 Add the tomatoes, olives and capers to the bowl, and gently mix to combine.

3 To make the dressing, put the mayonnaise in a bowl and whisk in the ajvar and vinegar.

4 Spoon the dressing over the salad and gently mix to combine. Serve sprinkled with the oregano.

Ajvar is a roasted capsicum (bell pepper) relish. It sometimes contains eggplant (aubergine). Buy ajvar from delicatessens and large supermarkets, or substitute it with a tomato or mixed vegetable relish.

Per serving
1411 kJ, 337 kcal, 23 g protein, 20 g fat (3 g saturated fat), 16 g carbohydrate (9 g sugars), 6 g fibre, 771 mg sodium

Creamy mushroom and quinoa salad

PREPARATION 10 minutes
COOKING 30 minutes
SERVES 2

2 tablespoons olive oil

1 small onion, finely chopped

400 g (14 oz) mushrooms, sliced

1 large zucchini (courgette), halved lengthwise and thickly sliced

1 large clove garlic, finely chopped

3–4 sprigs fresh thyme

1 tablespoon chopped fresh sage

½ cup (100 g) quinoa

1 cup (250 ml) salt-reduced chicken stock

⅓ cup (80 ml) skim evaporated milk

1 tablespoon grated parmesan

1 Heat the olive oil in a large saucepan over medium heat and sauté the onion for 1 minute. Add the mushrooms, zucchini, garlic, thyme and sage, and cook, stirring occasionally, for 5 minutes.

2 Stir in the quinoa and chicken stock, then cover and simmer for 15 minutes.

3 Stir in the milk and parmesan. Cover and simmer for a further 5 minutes. Serve hot.

High in protein, fibre, vitamins and minerals, quinoa (pronounced 'keen-wah') is highly nutritious, with a mild flavour. Button, shiitake, oyster and Swiss brown mushrooms all work well in this dish.

Per serving
*1992 kJ, 476 kcal, 22 g protein, 23 g fat
(4 g saturated fat), 46 g carbohydrate
(9 g sugars), 10 g fibre, 428 mg sodium*

Corn and capsicum salad with potatoes

PREPARATION 5 minutes
COOKING 15 minutes
SERVES 4

8 small new potatoes, halved lengthwise
2 corn cobs
2 slices bacon, rind removed, finely chopped
1 red capsicum (bell pepper), finely chopped
½ cup (40 g) fetta marinated in oil and herbs

1 Bring a large saucepan of water to a boil over high heat. Add the potatoes and cook for 12–15 minutes, until tender, then drain.

2 Meanwhile, stand each corn cob upright on a chopping board. Cut down the sides with a sharp knife to remove the kernels. Place the kernels in a large frying pan with 1/2 cup (125 ml) water and cook over medium–high heat for 3–4 minutes, until softened. Drain well.

3 Reheat the frying pan over high heat and cook the bacon and capsicum, stirring occasionally, for 4–5 minutes. Stir in the corn.

4 Place the potatoes on a platter and top with the corn mixture. Crumble the fetta over the top, drizzle with some of the marinating oil and serve.

For a creamier topping, stir some canned creamed corn through the corn mixture. Add sliced spring onions (scallions), blanched baby spinach leaves or chopped fresh parsley. Top with sour cream and grated cheddar instead of fetta.

Per serving
962 kJ, 230 kcal, 13 g protein, 6 g fat
(3 g saturated fat), 30 g carbohydrate
(3 g sugars), 6 g fibre, 376 mg sodium

Turkey and pomegranate salad

One of the joys of a roast turkey or chicken is the tender meat left over that is perfect for rustling up a super-quick meal. Add some basic fresh ingredients and perhaps a few special extras, and dinner is on the table.

PREPARATION 15 minutes
SERVES 4

1 red onion, halved and thinly sliced

100 g (3½ oz) watercress, trimmed

250 g (8 oz) mixed salad leaves

seeds of 1 pomegranate

⅓ cup (40 g) chopped pecans or walnuts

75 g (2½ oz) blue cheese (such as stilton), finely crumbled

200 g (7 oz) cooked turkey or chicken, diced

100 g (3½ oz) cooked ham, diced

Dressing

⅓ cup (80 ml) olive oil

2 tablespoons balsamic vinegar

1 teaspoon sugar

1 To make the dressing, whisk the oil, balsamic vinegar and sugar in a large bowl.

2 Add the red onion, watercress and salad leaves to the dressing, and toss to combine. Scatter the pomegranate seeds over the salad. Sprinkle the pecans or walnuts and cheese over the top.

3 Divide the salad among four bowls, add the turkey or chicken and ham, and serve.

Replace the pomegranate seeds with 200 g (7 oz) fresh blueberries or seedless red grapes.

Per serving
1946 kJ, 465 kcal, 26 g protein, 35 g fat (8 g saturated fat), 14 g carbohydrate (13 g sugars), 3 g fibre, 712 mg sodium

Duck salad with buckwheat

Chargrilled duck and vegetables are served on a bed
of salad leaves, herbs and toasted buckwheat. The duck
and vegetables could also be cooked on the barbecue.

PREPARATION 20 minutes

COOKING 35 minutes

SERVES 4

450 g (15 oz) boneless duck breasts,
skin and fat removed

¼ cup (60 ml) olive oil

2 cloves garlic, chopped

juice of 1 lemon

1 tablespoon chopped fresh rosemary

12 sprigs fresh thyme

1¼ cups (240 g) buckwheat

3 cups (750 ml) salt-reduced chicken
stock

125 g (4 oz) thin green beans

4 cups (200 g) mixed salad leaves

5 sprigs fresh basil, finely shredded

½ red onion, thinly sliced

8 pitted green olives

8 pitted black olives

2 zucchini (courgettes), thinly sliced
lengthwise

12 small spring onions (scallions),
trimmed

12 red cherry tomatoes

1½ tablespoons red wine vinegar,
or a mixture of sherry and balsamic
vinegars

freshly ground black pepper

Per serving
*2393 kJ, 572 kcal, 36 g protein, 22 g fat
(4 g saturated fat), 56 g carbohydrate
(10 g sugars), 7 g fibre, 663 mg sodium*

1 Using a sharp knife, score the duck flesh in a criss-cross pattern on both sides. Put the duck breasts in a bowl with 1 tablespoon of the olive oil, two-thirds of the garlic, the lemon juice, rosemary and half the thyme sprigs. Leave to marinate while you prepare the rest of the ingredients.

2 Toast the buckwheat kernels in a heavy-based frying pan over medium heat, stirring and tossing, for 4–5 minutes, until they are darker in colour. Remove from the heat.

3 Bring the stock to a boil in a saucepan, then stir in the buckwheat. Return to a boil, then reduce the heat, cover and cook over low heat for 10–15 minutes, until the stock has been absorbed and the buckwheat is tender. Remove from the heat and set aside, covered.

4 Heat a chargrill pan for 10 minutes. Meanwhile, blanch the beans in a saucepan of boiling water for 1–2 minutes. Drain and refresh under cold running water. Cut in half and add to a large salad bowl with the salad leaves, basil, onion and olives, and toss to mix.

5 Place the duck in the hot chargrill pan. Cook for 3 minutes, then turn and cook for a further 3 minutes (the meat will be rare, so cook longer if you prefer it well done). Transfer to a board. Place the zucchini, spring onions and tomatoes in the pan and cook for 1–2 minutes, until lightly charred.

6 Whisk the remaining olive oil and garlic with the vinegar and the leaves from the remaining thyme sprigs in a bowl, then drizzle over the salad. Spoon on the buckwheat, and arrange the hot zucchini, spring onions and tomatoes on top. Season with freshly ground black pepper. Slice the duck and serve on top of the salad.

Thai beef and broccoli salad

This wonderful Thai salad with fresh mint, basil, coriander and lime makes a perfect light lunch or dinner. The tender lean steak works perfectly with the crisp crunch of lightly steamed broccoli.

PREPARATION 10 minutes,
 plus 10 minutes marinating
COOKING 10 minutes
SERVES 4

500 g (1 lb) lean rump (round) steak

2 tablespoons lime juice

1½ tablespoons salt-reduced soy sauce

2 cloves garlic, crushed

1 cup (60 g) small broccoli florets

½ telegraph (long) cucumber, halved lengthwise and sliced

⅓ cup (7 g) fresh mint

⅓ cup (10 g) fresh basil

¼ cup (7 g) fresh coriander (cilantro) leaves

Lime and chilli dressing

2 tablespoons lime juice

1½ tablespoons salt-reduced soy sauce

2 long red chillies, seeded and sliced

2 teaspoons soft brown sugar

1 Put the steak in a large bowl with the lime juice, soy sauce and garlic. Turn to coat in the marinade, then set aside for 10 minutes.

2 Heat a chargrill pan or large non-stick frying pan over high heat. Cook the steak for 1–2 minutes on each side for rare, or until done to your liking. Set aside to cool.

3 Steam the broccoli in a steamer set over a saucepan of boiling water for 5–6 minutes, until just tender. Refresh immediately in cold water, then drain and allow to cool. Place in a large bowl with the cucumber and herbs.

4 Thinly slice the steak and add it to the salad.

5 To make the dressing, combine the lime juice, soy sauce, chillies and sugar in a small bowl.

6 Pour the dressing over the steak and broccoli, gently tossing to combine. Divide the salad among four plates and serve.

When broccoli is overcooked it loses both flavour and nutritional value, so steaming it is the best method to retain its excellent health benefits. Broccoli contains high levels of vitamins A, C and K, as well as fibre and folate.

Per serving
*801 kJ, 191 kcal, 29 g protein, 6 g fat
(3 g saturated fat), 5 g carbohydrate
(3 g sugars), 2 g fibre, 618 mg sodium*

Roquefort and pear salad

The pears, watercress and blue cheese are perfectly complemented by the subtle walnut oil dressing. Lightly toasted walnut pieces add crunch and extra flavour. Serve the salad with grainy wholemeal rolls for a tempting lunch.

PREPARATION 15 minutes

COOKING 5 minutes

SERVES 4

½ cup (60 g) walnut pieces

1 red onion, thinly sliced

3 large, ripe pears, preferably red-skinned

3¾ cups (115 g) watercress, trimmed

120 g (4 oz) roquefort or other blue cheese, crumbled

freshly ground black pepper

Poppyseed dressing

2 teaspoons red wine vinegar

½ teaspoon dijon mustard

freshly ground black pepper

1 tablespoon canola oil

1 tablespoon walnut oil

2 teaspoons poppyseeds

1 To make the dressing, stir the vinegar and mustard in a salad bowl and season with freshly ground black pepper. Gradually whisk in the oils, then stir in the poppyseeds. Set aside while you prepare the salad.

2 Lightly toast the walnut pieces in a small dry frying pan, stirring frequently until fragrant. Leave to cool.

3 Add the red onion to the bowl and mix with the dressing. Quarter, core and slice the pears, leaving the skin on. Add to the bowl and gently toss so that the pears are well coated with the dressing.

4 Add the watercress and most of the cheese and walnuts to the salad. Gently toss, then scatter over the remaining cheese and nuts, and serve immediately.

Other blue cheeses, such as stilton or Danish blue, work equally well here. As most blue cheeses are fairly salty, it isn't necessary to season the salad with salt.

Per serving
1603 kJ, 383 kcal, 10 g protein, 29 g fat
(7 g saturated fat), 21 g carbohydrate
(15 g sugars), 5 g fibre, 577 mg sodium

Sugarsnap pea, grape and fetta salad

Sugarsnap peas work well with baby spinach leaves and a little peppery rocket to provide the salad base for tangy fetta and sweet red grapes. Serve this quick lunch dish with thick slices of wholegrain bread or wholemeal pita bread.

PREPARATION 20 minutes
COOKING 1 minute
SERVES 4

300 g (10 oz) sugarsnap peas, halved

200 g (7 oz) seedless red or black grapes, halved

200 g (7 oz) fetta, cut into thin strips

45 g (1½ oz) rocket (arugula), shredded

170 g (6 oz) baby spinach leaves

Lemon dressing

grated zest and juice of ½ lemon

½ teaspoon caster (superfine) sugar

½ teaspoon dijon mustard

freshly ground black pepper

1 tablespoon extra virgin olive oil

1 To make the dressing, put the lemon zest and juice in a large salad bowl. Add the sugar and mustard, and season with freshly ground black pepper. Whisk until the sugar has dissolved in the lemon juice. Whisk in the olive oil.

2 Add the sugarsnap peas to a large saucepan of boiling water. Bring back to a boil, then immediately drain the sugarsnap peas and refresh under cold running water. Add the sugarsnap peas to the salad bowl, and turn and fold to coat them with the dressing.

3 Add the grapes, fetta, rocket and spinach to the bowl. Mix the salad gently but well, so that all the ingredients are coated with the dressing. Serve at once.

Instead of rocket, add 6 chopped spring onions (scallions). For a garlicky dressing, add 1 finely chopped garlic clove with the sugar and mustard. Add extra crunch by sprinkling the salad with 2 tablespoons toasted pine nuts just before serving.

Per serving
1070 kJ, 256 kcal, 12 g protein, 17 g fat (8 g saturated fat), 13 g carbohydrate (11 g sugars), 3 g fibre, 573 mg sodium

Great meals with a **bag** of **salad**

There's a huge variety of ready-to-eat prepared salad leaves at the supermarket. Rather than just serving them on the side, let them take the leading role. Here are four ideas for different occasions, all made in record time.

Smoked fish salad

PREPARATION 10 minutes • COOKING 10 minutes • SERVES 4

Cook **3 eggs** in a saucepan of boiling water for 10 minutes. Drain and place in a bowl of cold water to cool, then peel and cut into quarters. Arrange **200 g (7 oz) mixed salad leaves** on a serving platter. Skin **350 g (12 oz) smoked mackerel or other smoked fish** and break into large flakes. Toss **1 chopped red apple** in **2 teaspoons lemon juice.** Add the fish, apple and eggs to the salad. Mix ½ **cup (125 g) good-quality mayonnaise** with **2 teaspoons lemon juice** and drizzle over the salad. Grind over a little **black pepper.** Serve with triangles of buttered wholemeal (whole-wheat) bread.

Per serving *1247 kJ, 298 kcal, 28 g protein, 15 g fat (2 g saturated fat), 13 g carbohydrate (11 g sugars), 2 g fibre, 977 mg sodium*

Barbecued chicken and bacon salad

PREPARATION 5 minutes • COOKING 15 minutes • SERVES 4

Fry **200 g (7 oz) bacon pieces** in a dry frying pan until golden and crisp, then drain on paper towel. Scissor-snip **2 slices white bread** into small squares. Add to the hot fat in the pan with **1–2 tablespoons olive oil,** if necessary, and fry over medium–high heat until golden. Drain on paper towel. Whisk **2 tablespoons olive oil** and **2 teaspoons balsamic vinegar** in a large salad bowl. Add **240 g (8 oz) skinless barbecued chicken breast strips,** and toss to coat in the dressing. Add **135 g (4½ oz) watercress, baby spinach and rocket (arugula) salad,** and toss again. Scatter with the bacon and croutons, and serve.

Per serving *1178 kJ, 281 kcal, 20 g protein, 20 g fat (3 g saturated fat), 7 g carbohydrate (<1 g sugars), 1 g fibre, 210 mg sodium*

Curried chickpea salad

PREPARATION 10 minutes • **COOKING** 10 minutes • **SERVES 4**

Place **150 g (5 oz) mixed salad leaves,** such as frisée, baby spinach and rocket (arugula) in a bowl. Cube **1 large avocado** and toss with **1 teaspoon lemon juice.** Dice a **5 cm (2 inch) piece of cucumber** and halve **300 g (10 oz) red cherry tomatoes.** Toss the avocado, cucumber and tomatoes with the salad leaves. Heat **1½ tablespoons olive oil** in a non-stick frying pan. Cook **1 thinly sliced red onion** for 5 minutes, until tender and beginning to brown. Stir in ½ **teaspoon ground cumin, 1 teaspoon ground coriander, a pinch of ground turmeric** and a rinsed and drained **400 g (14 oz) can chickpeas.** Cook, stirring constantly, for 1–2 minutes, until the spices are fragrant. Remove from the heat and stir in **2 teaspoons lemon juice.** Cool for 2 minutes, then add to the salad and toss together until well combined. Make a simple minted yogurt dressing by stirring **2 teaspoons mint sauce** into **150 g (5 oz) natural (plain) yogurt.** Drizzle the dressing over the salad and serve with warmed naan.

Per serving *1111 kJ, 265 kcal, 8 g protein, 20 g fat (4 g saturated fat), 15 g carbohydrate (6 g sugars), 6 g fibre, 198 mg sodium*

Stir-fried teriyaki steak salad

PREPARATION 10 minutes • **COOKING** 2 minutes • **SERVES 4**

Trim **300 g (10 oz) thick-cut lean sirloin or rump (round) steak** of fat and cut into thin strips across the grain. Toss with **1 tablespoon teriyaki marinade.** If time permits, marinate in the fridge for 2 hours. Mix **150 g (5 oz) baby leaf and rocket (arugula) salad** with **1 thinly sliced yellow capsicum (bell pepper).** Divide the salad among four serving plates. Heat **1 tablespoon olive oil** in a heavy-based non-stick frying pan and swirl to coat the base. Stir-fry the steak for 1 minute, until browned on the outside but still pink inside. Add ¼ **cup (60 ml) teriyaki marinade** and **1 tablespoon water.** Quickly swirl the pan to coat the steak, then spoon onto the salad. Serve at once, with bread.

Per serving *861 kJ, 206 kcal, 17 g protein, 10 g fat (3 g saturated fat), 13 g carbohydrate (10 g sugars), <1 g fibre, 461 mg sodium*

Winter

Cold winter days make warm main meal salads appealing, as well as colourful side salads that sit alongside the season's heavy casseroles and stews – beetroot, cabbage, celeriac, potatoes and olives make their appearance, as well as apples and citrus fruits.

Prosciutto, pear and parmesan salad

PREPARATION 10 minutes
SERVES 2

1 cup (45 g) baby rocket (arugula)

1 pear, cored and thinly sliced

4 slices prosciutto, about 40 g (1½ oz)

¼ cup (30 g) shaved parmesan

Dressing

1 tablespoon olive oil

2 teaspoons balsamic vinegar

salt

freshly ground black pepper

1 Place the rocket and pear slices in a serving bowl. Tear the prosciutto into pieces and add to the bowl together with the parmesan. Gently toss to combine.

2 To make the dressing, whisk the oil and balsamic vinegar in a small bowl, and season with salt and freshly ground black pepper.

3 Drizzle the dressing over the salad and serve at once.

Stir-fry the prosciutto until crisp, then break it into pieces over the salad, or use pancetta instead.

Per serving
*1062 kJ, 254 kcal, 12 g protein, 17 g fat
(6 g saturated fat), 13 g carbohydrate
(10 g sugars), 2 g fibre, 484 mg sodium*

Buckwheat and cranberry salad

Dried cranberries and toasted pistachios are mixed with
buckwheat and dressed with a lemon and parsley dressing
in this nutritious salad, perfect with barbecued meats.

PREPARATION 10 minutes,
 plus 5 minutes standing
COOKING 15 minutes
SERVES 4

2 tablespoons pistachios

1 cup (190 g) roasted buckwheat

⅔ cup (80 g) dried cranberries

1 tablespoon extra virgin olive oil

¼ cup (60 ml) lemon juice

¼ cup (7 g) chopped fresh flat-leaf
 parsley

1 Preheat the oven to 180°C (350°F/Gas 4). Spread the
pistachios on a baking tray and bake for 3–5 minutes,
until lightly toasted. Cool slightly, then roughly chop.

2 Pour 1½ cups (375 ml) water into a saucepan, cover
and bring to a boil over high heat. Reduce the heat to
low, quickly add the buckwheat and replace the lid.
Gently simmer for 10 minutes, then turn off the heat,
briefly uncover the pan and stir in the cranberries.
Cover and allow to stand for 5 minutes.

3 Transfer the buckwheat mixture to a large bowl and
allow to cool slightly, stirring occasionally to release
the heat.

4 Add the oil, lemon juice, parsley and pistachios to the
bowl. Combine until well combined, then serve.

High in protein and nutrients, buckwheat
isn't actually a variety of wheat at all, and is
gluten-free. Roasted buckwheat (sometimes
known as 'kasha') has a nuttier flavour than
ordinary buckwheat. You'll find buckwheat
in health-food stores and the health-food
aisle of larger supermarkets.

Per serving
*1192 kJ, 284 kcal, 7 g protein, 5 g fat
(1 g saturated fat), 52 g carbohydrate
(14 g sugars), 3 g fibre, 8 mg sodium*

Red cabbage salad with apricots

This cabbage salad is an ideal winter side dish. It is a great variation of the usual apple and cabbage combination – the apricots add a lovely tart yet sweet flavour.

PREPARATION 20 minutes
COOKING 5 minutes
SERVES 4

1 red cabbage, about 500 g (1 lb)
⅓ cup (50 g) cashew nuts
8 soft dried apricots
fresh chives, to serve

Dressing
¼ cup (60 ml) apple juice
¼ cup (60 ml) cider vinegar
pinch of salt (optional)
freshly ground black pepper
¼ cup (60 ml) walnut oil

1 Remove the tough outer leaves from the cabbage. Quarter the cabbage and discard the hard stalk. Shred or thinly slice the cabbage, and place in a large salad bowl.

2 Toast the cashew nuts in a dry frying pan over medium heat until fragrant. Allow to cool slightly, then coarsely chop the cashews.

3 Put the dried apricots in a colander. Pour boiling water over the apricots, then drain and pat dry with paper towel. Roughly chop them and add to the cabbage along with the cashew nuts.

4 To make the dressing, whisk the apple juice, vinegar, salt, if using, and a little freshly ground black pepper in a small bowl. Whisk in the walnut oil.

5 Pour the dressing over the salad and gently toss until well combined. Serve garnished with chives.

Per serving
*1048 kJ, 250 kcal, 6 g protein, 19 g fat
(2 g saturated fat), 14 g carbohydrate
(11 g sugars), 7 g fibre, 29 mg sodium*

Witlof and watercress salad

PREPARATION 10 minutes

COOKING 5 minutes

SERVES 6

2 tablespoons sliced almonds

350 g (12 oz) watercress, trimmed

1 large head witlof (Belgian endive), halved lengthwise and thinly sliced

1 sweet red apple, halved, cored and thinly sliced

Yogurt dressing

⅓ cup (90 g) low-fat natural (plain) yogurt

1 tablespoon low-fat mayonnaise

2 teaspoons honey

1 teaspoon dijon mustard

¼ teaspoon curry powder

pinch of ground ginger

1 Toast the almonds in a small dry frying pan over medium heat, shaking the pan often, for 3–4 minutes, until they just begin to colour. Remove from the pan and cool completely before using.

2 Combine the watercress, witlof and apple in a large bowl.

3 To make the dressing, whisk the yogurt and mayonnaise with the honey, mustard, curry powder and ginger in a small bowl.

4 Drizzle the dressing over the salad and toss to combine. Sprinkle with the toasted almonds to serve.

Watercress and witlof are super sources of beta-carotene, while the almonds provide beneficial fats.

Per serving
*260 kJ, 62 kcal, 3 g protein, 2 g fat
(<1 g saturated fat), 7 g carbohydrate
(7 g sugars), 3 g fibre, 87 mg sodium*

Beetroot and fetta salad

PREPARATION 10 minutes
SERVES 2

6 canned baby beetroot (beets), about 200 g (7 oz)

1 cup (45 g) baby spinach leaves

½ cup (75 g) crumbled fetta

¼ cup (30 g) walnut pieces

Dressing

3 teaspoons olive oil

2 teaspoons red wine vinegar

1 teaspoon snipped fresh chives

salt

freshly ground black pepper

1 Drain the beetroot on paper towel and cut them into wedges. Gently toss the beetroot and spinach leaves together in a bowl.

2 Scatter the fetta and walnuts over the salad.

3 To make the dressing, whisk the oil, vinegar and chives in a small bowl, and season with salt and freshly ground black pepper.

4 Drizzle the dressing over the salad and serve.

This salad is fantastic with barbecued meats and crusty bread. Use marinated fetta, and use the oil from the fetta in the dressing.

Per serving
1271 kJ, 303 kcal, 10 g protein, 25 g fat
(7 g saturated fat), 10 g carbohydrate
(10 g sugars), 4 g fibre, 704 mg sodium

Kangaroo fillets with beetroot salad

Soft, tangy goat's cheese complements the beetroot and kangaroo beautifully, but it could be replaced with fetta. If you can only get large beetroot, cook them for 1 hour and then cut into small pieces once cooled. The kangaroo can be replaced with venison or beef.

PREPARATION 30 minutes,
 plus cooling
COOKING 15–45 minutes
SERVES 4

8 baby beetroot (beets) (400 g/14 oz in total), trimmed, small leaves reserved

2 kangaroo fillets (500 g/1 lb in total), about 2.5 cm (1 inch) thick

1 tablespoon olive oil

salt

freshly ground black pepper

1⅓ cups (60 g) baby or wild rocket (arugula)

75 g (2½ oz) soft goat's cheese, crumbled

1 tablespoon snipped fresh chives

Balsamic lemon dressing

1½ tablespoons balsamic vinegar

1 tablespoon lemon juice

1 tablespoon extra virgin olive oil

1 If you prefer cooked beetroot, cook in a large saucepan of boiling water for 30 minutes, until tender. Drain and set aside until just cool enough to handle. Slip off the skin and slice or cut each beetroot into eight wedges. Put in a bowl of iced water for at least 10 minutes. Drain, then dry with paper towel. If you prefer raw beetroot, peel and thinly slice with a mandolin or very sharp knife. Set aside.

2 Brush both sides of the kangaroo fillets with the olive oil and season with salt and freshly ground black pepper. Heat a large, heavy-based frying pan over medium–high heat. Cook the kangaroo for 5 minutes on each side for medium–rare and 6–7 minutes on each side for medium. Transfer to a warm plate, loosely cover with foil and rest for 5 minutes.

3 Put the beetroot in a large bowl with the beetroot leaves and rocket.

4 To make the dressing, whisk the vinegar, lemon juice and extra virgin olive oil in a small bowl.

5 Drizzle the dressing over the beetroot and salad leaves. Divide the salad among four serving plates, and scatter with the goat's cheese and chives. Slice the kangaroo across the grain, arrange on top of the salad and serve.

Per serving
1359 kJ, 325 kcal, 33 g protein, 17 g fat (6 g saturated fat), 10 g carbohydrate (10 g sugars), 3 g fibre, 361 mg sodium

Chicken liver salad

This dish provides the nutrient-rich benefits of liver, combined with the high levels of anti-oxidants found in oranges, parsley and many salad greens. You can buy different combinations of mixed salad leaves in packets at supermarkets and greengrocers.

PREPARATION 15 minutes

COOKING 30 minutes

SERVES 4

8 thin slices wholemeal (whole-wheat) bread, crusts removed

olive oil spray

2 large oranges

1 tablespoon olive oil

500 g (1 lb) chicken livers, sinew discarded, halved if large

½ cup (15 g) roughly chopped fresh flat-leaf parsley

freshly ground black pepper

125 g (4 oz) mixed salad leaves

1 Preheat the oven to 200°C (400°F/Gas 6). Line a large baking tray with baking (parchment) paper. Cut each bread slice into four small triangles. Place on the tray and spray with olive oil. Bake for 10–15 minutes, until the bread is crisp and golden. Set aside to cool.

2 Meanwhile, finely grate the zest of the oranges and set aside. Remove all skin and pith from the oranges. Using a small sharp knife, remove the segments from the oranges, working over a bowl to catch the juice. Put the segments on a plate and set the juice aside.

3 Heat 1 teaspoon of the olive oil in a non-stick frying pan over medium heat. Add one-quarter of the livers and cook for 1–2 minutes on each side, until they are browned and almost cooked through. Transfer the livers to a plate, cover and keep warm. Repeat with the remaining livers, cooking one-quarter at a time.

4 Return all the livers to the pan along with the orange zest and parsley. Toss for 1–2 minutes, until combined and heated through. Season with freshly ground black pepper, then remove from the heat.

5 Arrange the salad leaves and orange segments on four serving plates. Top with the chicken livers and place the toast triangles alongside. Whisk the remaining oil with the reserved orange juice. Drizzle over the salads just before serving.

Per serving
2188 kJ, 523 kcal, 35 g protein, 17 g fat (3 g saturated fat), 56 g carbohydrate (12 g sugars), 10 g fibre, 695 mg sodium

Potato, egg and bacon salad

There is no need to peel small new potatoes as they have very thin skins. Leaving the skin on helps retain flavour and also increases the fibre content. You can use left-over cooked potatoes, and add some baby spinach leaves for a complete meal.

PREPARATION 10 minutes
COOKING 20 minutes
SERVES 2

6–8 small new potatoes, about 300 g (10 oz) in total, halved

2 eggs

1 teaspoon olive oil

2 small slices bacon, rind removed, chopped

1 spring onion (scallion), sliced

salt

freshly ground black pepper

Creamy mustard dressing

2 tablespoons good-quality mayonnaise

1 tablespoon sour cream

1 teaspoon white wine vinegar

½ teaspoon dijon mustard

1 Put the potatoes in a saucepan, cover with cold water and bring to a boil. Cook for 10–15 minutes, until tender. Drain well and place in a large bowl.

2 Meanwhile, place the eggs in a small saucepan and cover with cold water. Bring to a boil, then cook for 10 minutes. Cool the eggs under cold running water, then peel and cut into quarters.

3 Heat the oil in a small non-stick frying pan over medium heat. Cook the bacon for 5 minutes, until crisp. Drain on paper towel and allow to cool.

4 To make the dressing, combine the mayonnaise, sour cream, vinegar and mustard in a bowl. Mix until smooth.

5 Add the dressing to the bowl with the potatoes, along with most of the bacon and spring onion. Season with salt and freshly ground black pepper, and gently toss to combine.

6 Top the salad with the eggs and sprinkle with the rest of the bacon and spring onion. Serve at room temperature, or cover and refrigerate until required.

Instead of using both mayonnaise and sour cream, just use one or the other. Replace the vinegar with lemon juice, and the spring onion with snipped fresh chives. Use prosciutto or salami instead of bacon.

Per serving
1489 kJ, 355 kcal, 20 g protein, 21 g fat (6 g saturated fat), 21 g carbohydrate (2 g sugars), 3 g fibre, 729 mg sodium

Lentil and sausage salad

Tiny green puy lentils have a slightly nutty texture and flavour. They keep their shape well once cooked, making them perfect in salads. Here they are mixed with sausages and Mediterranean vegetables, plus a handful of fresh rocket.

PREPARATION 30 minutes
COOKING 35 minutes
SERVES 6

1½ cups (300 g) French-style green (puy) lentils

2 red capsicums (bell peppers), halved lengthwise

4 zucchini (courgettes), halved lengthwise

¼ cup (60 ml) extra virgin olive oil

500 g (1 lb) good-quality sausages

2 small red or white onions, cut into wedges

2 stalks celery, thinly sliced

2 cloves garlic, thinly sliced

300 g (10 oz) new potatoes, scrubbed and diced

2 tablespoons chopped fresh thyme

⅓ cup (10 g) chopped fresh flat-leaf parsley

2 tablespoons sherry vinegar

1 tablespoon German or dijon mustard

salt

freshly ground black pepper

1 cup (45 g) rocket (arugula)

1 Rinse the lentils and add them to a large saucepan of water. Bring to a boil, then reduce the heat, cover and gently simmer for 25 minutes, until just tender. Drain, reserving a little of the cooking water.

2 While the lentils are cooking, preheat the grill (broiler) to high. Rub the skins of the capsicums and zucchini with a little of the oil. Arrange the vegetables, skin side up, in the grill pan in a single layer. Add the sausages and cook, turning the sausages occasionally, for 10–15 minutes, until the sausages are cooked and browned on all sides and the vegetables are tender. Transfer the capsicums to a plastic bag and leave until cool enough to handle, then remove from the bag and peel off the skins.

3 Heat the remaining oil in a large frying pan and add the onions, celery, garlic and potatoes. Cook, stirring, for about 10 minutes, until tender.

4 Roughly chop the sausages, capsicums and zucchini, then add them to the pan along with the lentils, thyme, parsley, vinegar and mustard. Stir well, adding a little of the lentil cooking water to slightly moisten the mixture. Season with salt and freshly ground black pepper.

5 Transfer the mixture to a serving bowl and serve warm or cool, tossing with the rocket just before serving.

Per serving
2123 kJ, 507 kcal, 25 g protein, 32 g fat (12 g saturated fat), 32 g carbohydrate (4 g sugars), 12 g fibre, 778 mg sodium

Apple and fennel salad with blue cheese dressing

This is a tasty salad to have in your repertoire for the winter months. Bulb fennel has a distinctive, sweet aniseed flavour that works well with bitter witlof and refreshing crisp apple. A creamy blue cheese dressing is the perfect partner.

PREPARATION 15 minutes
COOKING 2 minutes
SERVES 4

¼ cup (30 g) hazelnuts

1 large bulb fennel, thinly sliced

1 large head witlof (Belgian endive), shredded crosswise

2 red apples

100 g (3½ oz) radicchio rosso leaves

2 tablespoons snipped fresh chives

Blue cheese dressing

50 g (1¾ oz) blue cheese, such as Danish blue, crumbled

2 tablespoons tepid water

⅓ cup (90 g) low-fat natural (plain) yogurt

freshly ground black pepper

1 Heat a small non-stick frying pan over high heat. Add the hazelnuts and toast, stirring frequently, for 2 minutes, until fragrant. Immediately tip the hazelnuts out onto a clean tea towel (dish towel) and rub them to remove the papery skins. Coarsely chop the nuts and set aside.

2 To make the dressing, combine the blue cheese and water in a large bowl and mash to a smooth paste using the back of a spoon. Stir in the yogurt to make a thick, fairly smooth dressing. Season with freshly ground black pepper.

3 Stir the fennel and witlof into the dressing. Core and thinly slice the apples, then add to the bowl. Gently toss to coat with the dressing. Fold in the hazelnuts.

4 Arrange the radicchio leaves on four plates. Top with the salad and sprinkle with the chives. Serve at once.

 You can toast the hazelnuts beforehand and store them in an airtight container. Prepare the dressing several hours in advance and refrigerate it until you are ready to assemble the salad.

Per serving
662 kJ, 158 kcal, 6 g protein, 9 g fat (3 g saturated fat), 14 g carbohydrate (12 g sugars), 4 g fibre, 183 mg sodium

Bean sprout salad

The nutritional content of pulses and grains dramatically increases when they are sprouted – there is 60 per cent more vitamin C and almost 30 per cent more B vitamins found in the sprout than in the original seed. Choose crisp, fresh-looking sprouts, preferably with the seed still attached.

PREPARATION 25 minutes,
  plus 1 hour soaking
SERVES 4

¼ cup (45 g) dried apricots, chopped

125 g (4 oz) dried mango, chopped

⅓ cup (80 ml) apple juice

2 zucchini (courgettes), diced

2 small heads witlof (Belgian endive), halved lengthwise and sliced

3⅓ cups (300 g) assorted sprouts, such as mung bean, adzuki beans and alfalfa

Ginger and honey dressing

30 g (1 oz) piece fresh ginger, peeled and finely chopped

1 teaspoon wholegrain mustard

2 teaspoons cider vinegar

2 teaspoons honey

salt

freshly ground black pepper

¼ cup (60 ml) sunflower or vegetable oil

1 tablespoon poppyseeds

1 Put the dried apricots and mango in a salad bowl and spoon over the apple juice. Cover and leave to soak for 1 hour, until the juice has been absorbed and the dried fruit is plump.

2 Add the zucchini, witlof and sprouts to the bowl, and toss together to combine well.

3 To make the dressing, first press the ginger in a garlic press to give 2 teaspoons of juice. Whisk the ginger juice with the mustard, vinegar and honey, and season with salt and freshly ground black pepper. Gradually add the oil, whisking until slightly thickened. Stir in the poppyseeds.

4 Pour the dressing over the salad, toss and serve at once.

Dried fruit is a concentrated source of nutrients, including iron, phosphorus, calcium and some B vitamins. It is also a great source of dietary fibre. Although only a small quantity is used in this recipe, poppyseeds make a contribution to the protein content of this salad.

Per serving
*1240 kJ, 296 kcal, 6 g protein, 16 g fat
(2 g saturated fat), 33 g carbohydrate
(30 g sugars), 7 g fibre, 186 mg sodium*

Roast beef and rice salad

This rice salad is packed with vitamins, minerals and fibre. It is an excellent way of using up left-over roast beef, and the vegetables can be varied to suit all tastes. It also works well with brown rice, although the cooking time will be longer.

PREPARATION 25 minutes, plus
  at least 30 minutes marinating
  and chilling
COOKING 10 minutes
SERVES 4

500 g (1 lb) roast beef, preferably
  cooked medium–rare or medium,
  trimmed of fat and cut into cubes

⅓ cup (50 g) sun-dried tomatoes in oil,
  drained and thinly sliced

4 spring onions (scallions), thinly sliced

2 tablespoons snipped fresh chives

1¼ cups (250 g) basmati rice, rinsed

1 stalk celery, thinly sliced

1 carrot, coarsely grated

1 zucchini (courgette), coarsely grated

75 g (2½ oz) button mushrooms,
  thinly sliced

⅓ cup (10 g) chopped fresh flat-leaf
  parsley

radicchio rosso or other salad leaves,
  to serve

Cider vinegar dressing
1½ teaspoons mustard powder
½ teaspoon caster (superfine) sugar
2 tablespoons cider vinegar
¼ cup (60 ml) extra virgin olive oil
salt
freshly ground black pepper

1 To make the dressing, put the mustard powder and sugar in a large bowl and stir in the vinegar until smooth. Whisk in the oil until thoroughly blended. Season with salt and freshly ground black pepper.

2 Add the cubed beef, sun-dried tomatoes, spring onions and chives to the bowl, and stir to coat with the dressing. Cover and chill for at least 30 minutes (or up to 8 hours).

3 While the beef is marinating, cook the rice in a saucepan of boiling water for 8–10 minutes, until just tender. Drain well and spread out on a tray to cool completely.

4 Transfer the cooled rice to a bowl and stir in the celery, carrot, zucchini, mushrooms and parsley. Cover with plastic wrap and chill until required.

5 About 10 minutes before serving, remove the marinated beef and the rice salad from the refrigerator. Line four plates with radicchio or other salad leaves. Add the beef mixture to the rice salad and gently stir until well mixed. Spoon the salad onto the bed of leaves and serve.

Per serving
2791 kJ, 667 kcal, 48 g protein, 27 g fat
(8 g saturated fat), 56 g carbohydrate
(7 g sugars), 4 g fibre, 266 mg sodium

Potato and horseradish salad

PREPARATION 15 minutes
COOKING 10 minutes
SERVES 8

1 kg (2 lb) small new potatoes or kipfler (fingerling) potatoes
2 small heads witlof (Belgian endive), leaves separated
½ cup (15 g) chopped fresh flat-leaf parsley
2 tablespoons roughly chopped fresh tarragon
½ cup (60 g) roughly chopped walnuts

Horseradish dressing
juice of 1 lemon
1 tablespoon grated fresh horseradish root
200 g (7 oz) crème fraîche or sour cream
pinch of sea salt

1 Cut the potatoes in half and cook in a large saucepan of boiling water for 10 minutes, until tender. Drain, then briefly cool.

2 Place the potatoes in a large bowl. Add the witlof, parsley, tarragon and walnuts, and toss to combine.

3 To make the dressing, combine the lemon juice, grated horseradish and crème fraîche or sour cream in a small bowl. Season with sea salt.

4 Pour the dressing over the salad and toss to combine.

This crunchy potato salad goes well with barbecued meats. Adding the dressing while the potatoes are still warm means they will absorb the flavours of the dressing. Fresh horseradish roots can be grated and frozen. Grating releases their pungent volatile oil.

Per serving
986 kJ (236 kcal), 5 g protein, 16 g fat
(8 g saturated fat), 18 g carbohydrate
(2 g sugars), 3 g fibre, 96 mg sodium

Potato and lentil salad

PREPARATION 15 minutes
COOKING 20 minutes
SERVES 6

1 kg (2 lb) boiling (waxy) potatoes, scrubbed

¼ cup (60 ml) olive oil

2 tablespoons red wine vinegar

400 g (14 oz) can brown lentils, rinsed and drained well

1¼ cups (150 g) pitted black olives

1 tablespoon capers, rinsed and squeezed dry, chopped

2 cloves garlic, chopped

¼ cup (7 g) roughly chopped fresh flat-leaf parsley

6 spring onions (scallions), diagonally sliced

1 tablespoon lemon juice

salt

freshly ground black pepper

1 Cut the potatoes into large chunks, leaving the skin on. Add to a large saucepan of boiling water and cook for 15–20 minutes, until tender. Drain and transfer the potatoes to a large bowl.

2 Stir the olive oil and vinegar through the hot potatoes. Add the lentils, olives, capers, garlic, parsley, spring onions and lemon juice. Season with a pinch of salt and a good grinding of black pepper. Toss well to combine and serve warm.

Potatoes and lentils make great partners, with their earthiness and ability to carry other flavours.

Per serving
*1015 kJ, 243 kcal, 7 g protein, 11 g fat
(2 g saturated fat), 27 g carbohydrate
(2 g sugars), 4 g fibre, 510 mg sodium*

Asian-style apple and sprout salad

In this crunchy raw salad, apple, carrot, celery and sprouts are tossed with sunflower seeds and dressed with a fresh lime, ginger and coriander dressing.

PREPARATION 15 minutes
SERVES 4

1 carrot, cut into thin matchsticks

1 stalk celery, cut into thin matchsticks

1 red apple, cored, quartered and thinly sliced

1 cup (90 g) bean sprouts, trimmed

¾ cup (45 g) alfalfa sprouts

½ cup (60 g) sunflower seeds

Lime and ginger dressing

2 tablespoons sunflower oil

½ teaspoon sesame oil

1 tablespoon lime juice

½ teaspoon salt-reduced soy sauce

1 tablespoon chopped fresh coriander (cilantro) leaves

1 teaspoon grated fresh ginger

freshly ground black pepper

1 Combine the carrot, celery, apple, bean sprouts, alfalfa sprouts and sunflower seeds in a large bowl, and toss well to combine.

2 To make the dressing, whisk the oils, lime juice, soy sauce, coriander and ginger in a small bowl. Season with freshly ground black pepper.

3 Just before serving, pour the dressing over the salad and toss well so that the ingredients are evenly coated.

For a more substantial salad or to serve as a light main dish, replace the bean sprouts with sprouted green or brown lentils. You can also add ½ cup (100 g) diced firm tofu that has been pan-fried in a little sunflower or vegetable oil.

Per serving
842 kJ, 201 kcal, 5 g protein, 18 g fat (2 g saturated fat), 7 g carbohydrate (6 g sugars), 4 g fibre, 44 mg sodium

Beetroot and mozzarella salad

The crimson-striped leaves and red and yellow baby beetroot in this salad provide colour and plenty of anti-oxidants. A horseradish dressing adds a little heat and pungency.

PREPARATION 20 minutes
SERVES 4

200 g (7 oz) beetroot (beet) leaves

1 small bunch (about 650 g/1 lb 5 oz) baby red beetroot (beets), trimmed and thinly sliced

1 small bunch (about 650 g/1 lb 5 oz) baby yellow beetroot (beets), trimmed and thinly sliced

1 Lebanese or other small cucumber, thinly sliced

2 fresh mozzarella, about 100 g (3½ oz) each, torn into bite-sized pieces

¼ cup (5 g) fresh mint

2 tablespoons fresh dill sprigs

Horseradish dressing

2 tablespoons olive oil

2 tablespoons lemon juice

1 teaspoon caster (superfine) sugar

2 teaspoons horseradish cream, from a jar

salt

freshly ground black pepper

1 Arrange the beetroot leaves, red and yellow beetroot, cucumber, mozzarella and herbs on a serving platter.

2 To make the dressing, put the oil, lemon juice, sugar and horseradish cream in a bowl. Season with salt and freshly ground black pepper, and whisk until well combined.

3 Drizzle the dressing over the salad and serve.

Gently wash the beetroot before slicing so that you don't pierce the thin skin. If you can't find yellow beetroot, just use 2 bunches of red beetroot.

Per serving
1352 kJ, 323 kcal, 18 g protein, 22 g fat (9 g saturated fat), 15 g carbohydrate (13 g sugars), 6 g fibre, 600 mg sodium

Minted barley and bean salad

This filling salad is a great choice for a satisfying lunch. Both barley and beans are low-glycaemic (GI) 'superfoods', creating a steady and slow increase in blood glucose levels that keeps you going between meals.

PREPARATION 1 hour 30 minutes
COOKING 45 minutes
SERVES 4

3 cups (750 ml) salt-reduced vegetable stock

1 strip lemon zest

1 bay leaf

250 g (8 oz) baby leeks, white part only

1 teaspoon canola oil

1 cup (220 g) pearl barley

400 g (14 oz) can salt-reduced black-eyed peas, rinsed and drained

6 roma (plum) tomatoes, about 500 g (1 lb) in total, cut into thin wedges

3 cups (135 g) baby spinach leaves, shredded

1 bunch (about 85 g/3 oz) spring onions (scallions), shredded

fresh mint sprig, to garnish

Dressing

2 sun-dried tomatoes in oil, drained and finely chopped, 2 tablespoons oil reserved

1 tablespoon red wine vinegar

1 clove garlic, crushed

2 tablespoons chopped fresh mint

1 tablespoon chopped fresh chervil

freshly ground black pepper

1 Put the stock and 2½ cups (625 ml) water in a saucepan with the lemon zest and bay leaf. Bring to a rapid boil, add the leeks and cook for 2–3 minutes, until just tender. Remove, drain and briefly refresh in cold water. Cut the leeks on the diagonal into short lengths. Set aside.

2 Add the canola oil to the hot stock in the pan and bring back to a boil. Add the barley, then cover and simmer for 30–40 minutes, until tender. Spoon out and reserve 2 tablespoons of the stock. Discard the lemon zest and bay leaf. Drain the barley, transfer to a bowl and set aside to cool.

3 Add the leeks, canned peas or beans, tomato wedges, spinach and spring onions to the barley, and gently stir to combine.

4 To make the dressing, put the sun-dried tomatoes, oil, vinegar, garlic, mint, chervil and reserved stock in a screw-top jar. Shake well until combined. Season with freshly ground black pepper.

5 Drizzle the dressing over the barley and vegetables, and toss until well coated. Serve at room temperature, garnished with a fresh mint sprig.

Per serving
1585 kJ, 379 kcal, 12 g protein, 13 g fat (2 g saturated fat), 53 g carbohydrate (10 g sugars), 13 g fibre, 827 mg sodium

Tuna and pink grapefruit salad

To vary this recipe, replace the pink grapefruit with the sweeter ruby red grapefruit, orange segments or diced fresh mango; or omit the grapefruit and add tomato wedges, black olives and fresh mint leaves.

PREPARATION 10 minutes
COOKING 10 minutes
SERVES 4

500 g (1 lb) fresh tuna or bonito fillets, skin removed

olive oil, for brushing

2 small pink grapefruit

2 small avocados, sliced

100 g (3½ oz) baby rocket (arugula)

Dressing
2 tablespoons white wine vinegar

¼ cup (60 ml) extra virgin olive oil

salt

freshly ground black pepper

1 Heat a frying pan over medium heat. Lightly brush the tuna fillets with olive oil and cook for 2–3 minutes on each side, until done to your liking. Remove from the pan and leave to cool, then slice or break into large chunks.

2 Meanwhile, cut the top and bottom off each grapefruit, and stand them on one cut end on a chopping board. Remove all skin and pith by cutting down around each grapefruit, to the chopping board. Segment the grapefruit by cutting out the flesh in wedges from between the membranes.

3 To make the dressing, whisk the vinegar and oil in a bowl, and season with salt and freshly ground black pepper.

4 Place the tuna, grapefruit segments, avocados, rocket and dressing in a large salad bowl. Gently toss together to combine, then serve immediately.

Instead of fresh tuna, use smoked trout, or canned tuna in a flavoured oil, and omit step 1.

Per serving
1708 kJ, 408 kcal, 34 g protein, 28 g fat (7 g saturated fat), 4 g carbohydrate (4 g sugars), 2 g fibre, 66 mg sodium

Chargrilled vegetable salad

This heart-healthy vegetable combination is tossed with a garlic and marjoram dressing. You can replace the fresh marjoram with dried marjoram and use half the amount.

PREPARATION 25 minutes

COOKING 20 minutes

SERVES 6

1 eggplant (aubergine), about 350 g (12 oz)

1 small bulb fennel, trimmed

1 yellow zucchini (courgette)

1 green zucchini (courgette)

¼ teaspoon salt

olive oil spray

1 small red capsicum (bell pepper), halved lengthwise

3 roma (plum) tomatoes, halved lengthwise and seeded

1½ tablespoons balsamic vinegar

Dressing

2 tablespoons olive oil

2 cloves garlic, crushed

1 teaspoon finely chopped fresh marjoram

¼ teaspoon salt

1 Preheat a barbecue or chargrill pan to medium–high. Cut the eggplant, fennel and zucchini lengthwise into 1 cm (½ inch) slices. Sprinkle with the salt and spray with oil.

2 Cook the capsicum, skin side down, for 3–4 minutes, until the skin is blackened and blistered. Set aside to cool.

3 Cook the eggplant, fennel and zucchini on one side for 4 minutes, until dark brown grill marks appear but the vegetables are still very firm. Turn over and cook until the vegetables are browned and just tender, 3 minutes for the zucchini and 5–6 minutes longer for the eggplant and fennel.

4 Spray the cut sides of the tomatoes with oil. Cook, cut side down, for 3 minutes, until light grill marks appear.

5 To make the dressing, heat the oil in a small frying pan over medium heat. Add the garlic, marjoram and salt, and sauté for 1 minute. Remove from the heat.

6 Peel the capsicum, cut into thin strips and transfer to a bowl. Cut the rest of the vegetables into chunks and add to the bowl along with the dressing and vinegar. Toss to coat, and serve at room temperature.

Per serving
394 kJ, 94 kcal, 2 g protein, 7 g fat (<1 g saturated fat), 6 g carbohydrate (5 g sugars), 4 g fibre, 221 mg sodium

Cabbage and bok choy salad with mini rice patties

The little rice patties make a novel and tasty topping for a crunchy salad of cabbage, Chinese greens and walnuts, brought together with a refreshing orange dressing.

PREPARATION 30 minutes
COOKING 25 minutes
SERVES 4

75 g (2½ oz) long-grain rice

200 ml (7 fl oz) vegetable stock

¼ red cabbage, about 250 g (8 oz), finely shredded

1 cup (125 g) walnut pieces, broken into smaller pieces if large

¼ cup (40 g) sesame seeds

1 egg, lightly beaten

salt

freshly ground black pepper

50 ml (1¾ fl oz) peanut (groundnut) oil

½ Chinese cabbage, about 300 g (10 oz), shredded

100 g (3½ oz) baby bok choy leaves, halved lengthwise if large

Orange dressing

50 ml (1¾ fl oz) peanut (groundnut) oil

juice of 1 orange

½ teaspoon grated orange zest

1 teaspoon soy sauce

salt

freshly ground black pepper

Per serving
2511 kJ, 600 kcal, 12 g protein, 52 g fat (7 g saturated fat), 23 g carbohydrate (7 g sugars), 7 g fibre, 701 mg sodium

1 Put the rice and stock in a saucepan and bring to a boil. Stir, cover and gently simmer for 10 minutes, until the rice is tender and has absorbed all the stock. Reduce the heat to low, uncover the rice and cook, stirring occasionally, for 1 minute, until slightly dry. Tip the rice into a bowl, spread out and leave to cool.

2 To make the dressing, add the oil, orange juice, orange zest and soy sauce to a large bowl. Season with salt and freshly ground black pepper, and whisk together.

3 Add the red cabbage to the dressing and toss well, then set aside to soften and marinate.

4 Toast the walnut pieces in a large, dry non-stick frying pan over medium heat, turning frequently, for 3 minutes, until golden. Tip onto a plate and set aside.

5 Stir the sesame seeds and egg into the rice, and season with salt and freshly ground black pepper. Heat the oil in the frying pan over medium–high heat. Drop teaspoons of the rice mixture into the pan and cook in batches for 2 minutes, until lightly browned. Turn over and cook the other side for 1½–2 minutes. Drain the patties on paper towel while you cook the remaining mixture.

6 Add the Chinese cabbage, bok choy and walnuts to the marinated red cabbage, and toss to coat in the dressing. Divide the salad among four plates and serve topped with the rice patties.

Middle Eastern lentil salad

This is a healthy and filling salad of lentils, capsicums and broccoli florets mixed with a lemon and coriander dressing, topped with dried apricots, goat's cheese and toasted sunflower seeds.

PREPARATION 20 minutes
COOKING 30 minutes
SERVES 4

1⅓ cups (250 g) green lentils, rinsed

1 clove garlic

large pinch of ground cumin

1 slice lemon

1 small red onion, finely chopped

½ cup (90 g) dried apricots, roughly chopped

1 small red capsicum (bell pepper), chopped

1 small yellow capsicum (bell pepper), chopped

1 small green capsicum (bell pepper), chopped

100 g (3½ oz) broccoli, broken into small florets

50 g (1¾ oz) firm rindless goat's cheese

2 tablespoons toasted sunflower seeds

Lemon and coriander dressing

juice of 1 lemon

¼ cup (60 ml) extra virgin olive oil

2 tablespoons finely chopped fresh coriander (cilantro)

salt

freshly ground black pepper

1 Put the lentils in a large saucepan, cover with water and bring to a boil, skimming off any scum. Add the peeled garlic clove, cumin and lemon, then reduce the heat and simmer for about 30 minutes, until the lentils are tender.

2 Meanwhile, to make the dressing, put the lemon juice, oil and coriander in a large salad bowl. Season with salt and freshly ground black pepper, and whisk well.

3 Drain the lentils, discarding the lemon and garlic. Add the lentils to the salad bowl and gently toss to combine with the dressing.

4 Add the onion, apricots, capsicums and broccoli florets, and gently mix. Crumble the cheese over the top, scatter over the sunflower seeds and serve immediately.

Like all pulses, lentils are a good source of soluble fibre, which can help to reduce high blood cholesterol levels. Lentils also offer protein, starchy carbohydrate and B vitamins. Dried apricots are an excellent source of beta-carotene as well as being a useful source of calcium.

Per serving
1704 kJ, 407 kcal, 21 g protein, 20 g fat (4 g saturated fat), 37 g carbohydrate (13 g sugars), 13 g fibre, 230 mg sodium

Chickpea and orange salad with tahini dressing

Serve this high-fibre salad with chargrilled chicken, fish or lamb cutlets. The salad can be made ahead if required and dressed close to serving time.

PREPARATION 10 minutes
COOKING 5 minutes
SERVES 4

400 g (14 oz) broccoli florets

1 orange

400 g (14 oz) can chickpeas, rinsed and drained

Tahini dressing

juice of 1 orange

2 tablespoons tahini

¼ teaspoon ground cumin, or to taste

salt

freshly ground black pepper

1 Cook the broccoli in a saucepan of boiling water for 2–3 minutes, until just cooked but still firm. Drain and refresh under cold running water, then drain again.

2 Cut the top and bottom off the orange, and stand on one cut end on a chopping board. Remove all skin and pith by cutting down around the orange, to the chopping board. Segment the orange by cutting out the flesh in wedges from between the membranes.

3 Add the orange segments, broccoli and chickpeas to a large salad bowl, and gently toss to combine.

4 To make the dressing, whisk the orange juice with the tahini and cumin. Season with salt and freshly ground black pepper.

5 Drizzle the dressing over the salad and serve.

 If the oranges are very sweet, you might like to whisk a squeeze of lemon juice into the dressing.

Per serving
725 kJ, 173 kcal, 11 g protein, 8 g fat (1 g saturated fat), 14 g carbohydrate (6 g sugars), 10 g fibre, 187 mg sodium

Coleslaw with celeriac, carrot and leek

Prepare the vegetables and dressing in advance and refrigerate until required. Toss everything to combine just before serving. For extra flavour and crunch, sprinkle the salad with mixed nuts or toasted sunflower seeds just before serving.

PREPARATION 20 minutes
SERVES 4

250 g (8 oz) celeriac

2 carrots

100 g (3½ oz) leek, white part only

Dressing

150 g (5 oz) low-fat mayonnaise

3 teaspoons lemon juice

2–3 teaspoons dijon mustard

freshly ground white pepper

salt

sugar, to taste

1 Peel and cut the celeriac and carrots into thin matchsticks. Trim the leek, halve lengthwise, wash and shake dry. Cut crosswise into fine strips with a large knife.

2 To make the dressing, whisk the mayonnaise, lemon juice and mustard in a large salad bowl until creamy. Season the dressing with plenty of freshly ground white pepper, salt and sugar.

3 Add the celeriac, carrots and leek to the dressing in the bowl. Toss to combine, and serve immediately.

Also known as celery root, celeriac tastes like a cross between celery and parsley. It can be eaten raw or cooked.

Per serving
393 kJ, 94 kcal, 2 g protein, 3 g fat (<1 g saturated fat), 15 g carbohydrate (12 g sugars), 5 g fibre, 627 mg sodium

Wilted spinach salad

PREPARATION 5 minutes
COOKING 5 minutes
SERVES 4

250 g (8 oz) baby spinach leaves

2 slices rindless, short-cut bacon, cooked and crumbled

2 slices wholegrain bread, trimmed, toasted and cut into small cubes

Warm tomato dressing

2 tablespoons olive oil

1 red onion, thinly sliced

¼ cup (60 ml) tomato juice

1 tablespoon lemon juice

1 teaspoon dijon mustard

1 small clove garlic, crushed

¼ teaspoon salt

pinch of freshly ground black pepper

Wholegrain bread is used in place of the usual white bread to make the croutons in this recipe.

1 Place the spinach in a large salad bowl.

2 To make the dressing, heat the oil in a large non-stick frying pan over medium heat. Sauté the onion for 1 minute. Stir in the tomato juice, lemon juice, mustard, garlic, salt and freshly ground black pepper. Heat until just boiling, then remove from the heat.

3 Pour the hot dressing over the spinach and toss to coat. Top the salad with the bacon and croutons. Serve warm.

Per serving
*712 kJ, 170 kcal, 7 g protein, 12 g fat
(2 g saturated fat), 9 g carbohydrate
(3 g sugars), 2 g fibre, 620 mg sodium*

Red cabbage and apple salad

PREPARATION 15 minutes
COOKING 25 minutes
SERVES 6

1 tablespoon olive oil
2 slices bacon, rind removed, chopped
1 small onion, finely chopped
¼ red cabbage, about 300 g (10 oz), shredded
2 green apples, peeled, cored and thinly sliced
1 tablespoon red wine vinegar
1 tablespoon soft brown sugar
salt
freshly ground black pepper

1 Heat the oil in a large saucepan over medium heat. Cook the bacon for 5 minutes, until lightly browned. Add the onion and sauté for 5 minutes, until the onion is soft.

2 Add the cabbage, apples and ¼ cup (60 ml) water to the pan and cook, stirring occasionally, for 15 minutes, until the cabbage is soft.

3 Stir in the vinegar and sugar. Season with salt and freshly ground black pepper, and serve warm.

This recipe also works with green cabbage, or a mixture of red and green cabbage. For a different flavour, add 1 teaspoon caraway seeds with the onion.

Per serving
402 kJ, 96 kcal, 4 g protein, 5 g fat
(<1 g saturated fat), 10 g carbohydrate
(9 g sugars), 3 g fibre, 323 mg sodium

Beetroot, rocket and goat's cheese salad

This vibrant salad is very simple yet very flavoursome. Instead of the crumbled goat's cheese you can also use crumbled fetta. When you are handling beetroot, it's a good idea to wear gloves to prevent your hands from being stained.

PREPARATION 10 minutes
SERVES 4

1¾ cups (60 g) wild rocket (arugula)

425 g (15 oz) can or jar of baby beetroot (beets)

1 large avocado, diced

75 g (2½ oz) goat's cheese

Dressing

1½ tablespoons extra virgin olive oil

3 teaspoons white wine vinegar

salt

freshly ground black pepper

1 Arrange the rocket in a shallow serving bowl.

2 Drain the beetroot well, then cut into halves or quarters. Arrange the beetroot and avocado on top of the rocket, then crumble the goat's cheese over the top.

3 To make the dressing, whisk the oil and vinegar in a small bowl. Season with salt and freshly ground black pepper.

4 Drizzle the dressing over the salad and serve.

For a beetroot and bean salad, substitute the rocket with 400 g (14 oz) lightly blanched baby green beans, replace the avocado with ⅓ cup (40 g) toasted slivered almonds, and use 175 g (6 oz) marinated fetta instead of goat's cheese. Whisk 2 tablespoons of the oil from the fetta with 1 tablespoon lemon juice and drizzle over the salad.

Per serving
*945 kJ, 226 kcal, 6 g protein, 19 g fat
(7 g saturated fat), 7 g carbohydrate
(7 g sugars), 3 g fibre, 297 mg sodium*

Warm potato salad

When buying potatoes, check how they are labelled. 'Boiling', 'waxy' or 'salad' potatoes are good for salads as they hold their shape when boiled. 'Starchy', 'floury', 'baking' or 'mashing' potatoes are best for roasting or mashing. 'All-purpose' potatoes are good all-rounders.

PREPARATION 10 minutes
COOKING 15 minutes
SERVES 4

500 g (1 lb) boiling (waxy) potatoes, such as desiree

2½ tablespoons olive oil

4 slices bacon, rind removed, diced

¼ cup (60 ml) white wine vinegar

2 tablespoons sugar

½ teaspoon salt

freshly ground black pepper

2 spring onions (scallions), thinly sliced

1 Cut the potatoes into chunks, leaving the skin on if preferred. Cook the potatoes in a saucepan of gently boiling water for 8–10 minutes, until just tender when pierced with a knife.

2 While the potatoes are cooking, heat 2 teaspoons of the oil in a non-stick frying pan over medium–high heat. Cook the bacon for 5 minutes, until crisp. Remove the bacon from the pan and set aside.

3 Add the vinegar, sugar, salt and some freshly ground black pepper to the frying pan and bring to a boil. Pour the mixture into a small heatproof bowl and whisk in the remaining oil.

4 Drain the potatoes and place in a large bowl. Add the spring onions, dressing and bacon, and gently toss to combine. Serve warm.

Substitute spicy chorizo sausage for the bacon, or toss through some chopped fresh flat-leaf parsley, thinly sliced celery, cooked green peas, or a diced green pear with the skin on.

Per serving
1213 kJ, 290 kcal, 12 g protein, 15 g fat
(3 g saturated fat), 25 g carbohydrate
(9 g sugars), 3 g fibre, 945 mg sodium

Tomato, olive and caper salad in baby cos leaves

You can simply stir the olives and capers into ready-made garlic aïoli to save time peeling and crushing the garlic. You won't need any anchovy paste if you are using aïoli.

PREPARATION 20 minutes
SERVES 4

2 baby cos (romaine) lettuces

100 g (3½ oz) red cherry tomatoes

90 g (3 oz) parmesan

Dressing

50 g (1¾ oz) mayonnaise

¼ cup (60 ml) olive oil

¼ cup (30 g) pitted black olives, chopped

2 tablespoons capers, rinsed and squeezed dry, chopped

1 small clove garlic, crushed

½–¾ teaspoon anchovy paste

1 Remove the outer leaves from the lettuces and place two leaves on each of four serving plates. Coarsely chop the lettuce hearts and divide among the leaves.

2 Halve or quarter the tomatoes, depending on size, and divide among the lettuce leaves.

3 To make the dressing, combine the mayonnaise and oil in a small bowl. Stir in the olives, capers and garlic. Add the anchovy paste, to taste.

4 Spoon the dressing over the tomatoes and lettuce. Shave or grate the parmesan on top and serve immediately.

If you are serving the salad as a side dish, arrange the lettuce leaves in a circle on a large platter.

Per serving
1203 kJ, 287 kcal, 10 g protein, 26 g fat (7 g saturated fat), 4 g carbohydrate (3 g sugars), 1 g fibre, 724 mg sodium

Duck and apple salad

Replace the duck with a boneless, skinless chicken breast, or use
a cooked Peking duck breast from the supermarket. You could also
use slices of left-over cooked turkey. Instead of apple slices, use
orange segments.

PREPARATION 10 minutes
COOKING 15 minutes
SERVES 2

2 small boneless duck breasts with skin

salt

freshly ground black pepper

1 cup (30 g) watercress sprigs

1 cup (30 g) shredded radicchio rosso

1 red apple, cored and thinly sliced

2 spring onions (scallions), diagonally
   sliced

Dressing

1 tablespoon olive oil

2 teaspoons white wine vinegar

salt

freshly ground black pepper

1. Preheat the oven to 190°C (375°F/Gas 5).

2. Place an ovenproof non-stick frying pan over medium–low heat. Season the duck breasts with salt and freshly ground black pepper, and place in the pan, skin side down. Cook for 6–8 minutes, until most of the fat has rendered and the skin is crisp. Turn and cook the other side for 1 minute.

3. Transfer the frying pan to the oven and cook the duck for 6 minutes for medium, or until done to your liking. Set the duck aside to rest for a few minutes, then thinly slice it.

4. Combine the watercress, radicchio, apple, spring onions and duck slices in a bowl.

5. To make the dressing, whisk the oil and vinegar in a small bowl. Season with salt and freshly ground black pepper.

6. Pour the dressing over the salad, gently toss together and serve immediately.

Per serving
1175 kJ, 281 kcal, 26 g protein, 14 g fat
(2 g saturated fat), 10 g carbohydrate
(9 g sugars), 2 g fibre, 85 mg sodium

Thai beef salad

To speed up the cooking time, slice the beef into thin strips, or to reduce the preparation time, buy the beef already cut into strips for stir-frying. For a bit of heat, add some seeded and finely chopped red chilli.

PREPARATION 20 minutes
COOKING 10 minutes
SERVES 4

500 g (1 lb) piece of rump (round) steak
vegetable oil, for brushing
3 carrots, about 90 g (3 oz) each
⅓ cup (10 g) fresh coriander (cilantro) leaves

Dressing
1½ tablespoons lime juice
3 teaspoons fish sauce

1 Heat a frying pan over medium–high heat. Lightly brush the steak with oil and cook for 2–3 minutes on each side for medium–rare, or until done to your liking. Remove from the pan and set aside to cool, reserving any pan juices for the dressing.

2 Peel the carrots, then use a food processor or shredder to cut them into thin julienne strips, or use a vegetable peeler to peel them into thin ribbons. Place the carrots in a large salad bowl.

3 Thinly slice the beef, then add to the carrots along with the coriander.

4 To make the dressing, whisk the lime juice with the fish sauce and any pan juices from the beef.

5 Drizzle the dressing over the salad, toss together and serve immediately.

Add 1–2 teaspoons sesame oil to the dressing, or sprinkle the salad with toasted sesame seeds.

Per serving
*716 kJ, 171 kcal, 28 g protein, 6 g fat
(2 g saturated fat), 2 g carbohydrate
(2 g sugars), 1 g fibre, 412 mg sodium*

Ways with potato salads

Potato salads are a great way to enjoy new potatoes or specialty salad potatoes. Be sure to use a boiling (waxy) variety so the potatoes keep their shape when they are cooked and combined with other ingredients.

Potato and smoked turkey salad

PREPARATION 15 minutes • COOKING 15 minutes • SERVES 6

Peel **1 kg (2 lb) red potatoes** and cut into 1 cm (½ inch) chunks. Cook in a large saucepan of boiling water for 10 minutes, until tender; drain well. Heat **1 tablespoon olive oil** in a large frying pan over medium heat. Sauté **1 large diced onion, 1 diced red capsicum (bell pepper)** and **1 diced green capsicum** for 5 minutes, until the capsicums are tender but still crisp. Place in a large salad bowl and whisk in **1 cup (250 ml) chicken stock, ¼ cup (60 ml) white vinegar, 1 tablespoon dijon mustard** and **½ teaspoon salt**. Add **60 g (2 oz) cubed smoked turkey** and the potatoes to the bowl. Toss and serve warm or chilled.

Per serving *751 kJ, 179 kcal, 9 g protein, 4 g fat (<1 g saturated fat), 26 g carbohydrate (4 g sugars), 4 g fibre, 525 mg sodium*

Potato and bacon salad

PREPARATION 10 minutes • COOKING 15 minutes • SERVES 4

Cook **5 chopped slices lean bacon** in a lightly oiled frying pan over high heat until crisp; drain on paper towel. Cook **1 kg (2 lb) small new potatoes** in a saucepan of boiling water for 15 minutes, until just tender. Drain, cut in half, and place in a large bowl while still warm. Add **4 quartered hard-boiled eggs, ½ cup (50 g) chopped pickled cucumbers** and **¼ cup (7 g) chopped fresh flat-leaf parsley**. Combine **⅔ cup (160 g) mayonnaise, ⅓ cup (90 g) sour cream, 1 tablespoon lemon juice** and **1 teaspoon paprika**. Gently toss with the salad. Top with the bacon and **2 tablespoons chopped fresh dill**.

Per serving *2268 kJ, 542 kcal, 25 g protein, 29 g fat (9 g saturated fat), 44 g carbohydrate (10 g sugars), 6 g fibre, 1261 mg sodium*

Potato and ham salad

PREPARATION 20 minutes • COOKING 15 minutes • SERVES 4

Peel and dice **750 g (1½ lb) boiling (waxy) potatoes** and cook until just soft. Drain, then briefly steam. Finely chop **5 cornichons or small gherkins (pickled cucumbers)** and **1 tablespoon rinsed capers**, and combine with **¾ cup (185 g/7 oz) mayonnaise** and **2 teaspoons mustard**. Thoroughly mix, adding some cornichon liquid if necessary. Season with **salt and freshly ground black pepper**. Add the potatoes. Finely chop or slice **4 stalks celery, 1 green capsicum (bell pepper)** and **1 onion**, and add to the bowl with **200 g (7 oz) finely diced ham**. Gently stir in **3 chopped hard-boiled eggs** and **12 pitted black olives**. Line a bowl with **cos (romaine) lettuce leaves** and arrange the salad on top. Serve garnished with **1 sliced hard-boiled egg**.

Per serving 1809 kJ, 432 kcal, 20 g protein, 22 g fat (4 g saturated fat), 38 g carbohydrate (10 g sugars), 5 g fibre, 1655 mg sodium

New potato salad
with herb cream

New potato salad with herb cream

PREPARATION 15 minutes • COOKING 10 minutes • SERVES 4

Cook **1 kg (2 lb) small new potatoes** in a saucepan of boiling water for 15 minutes, until just tender. Drain, return to the pan and shake over low heat for a few minutes to evaporate any moisture. Transfer to a bowl and leave to cool for 5 minutes. Sprinkle **1 teaspoon white wine vinegar** and **2 tablespoons dry white vermouth or dry white wine** over the potatoes. Season with **salt and freshly ground black pepper**, gently toss and set aside to cool completely. Dice **½ large cucumber** and add to the potatoes with **4 thinly sliced spring onions (scallions)**, **¼ cup (15 g) chopped fresh dill** and **1½ tablespoons chopped fresh tarragon**. Combine **1 finely chopped clove garlic**, **¼ cup (60 g) low-fat mayonnaise** and **100 g (3½ oz) low-fat natural (plain) yogurt**. Spoon the dressing over the potatoes and gently combine. Serve the salad at room temperature or chilled, garnished with **chopped fresh dill and tarragon leaves**.

Per serving 957 kJ, 229 kcal, 8 g protein, 3 g fat (<1 g saturated fat), 39 g carbohydrate (6 g sugars), 6 g fibre, 291 mg sodium

Index

Notes to the reader

ALTERNATIVE TERMS AND SUBSTITUTES

baby cos lettuce – little gem, romaine

burghul – bulgur

butterbeans – lima beans

capsicum – bell pepper, sweet pepper

coriander – cilantro

corn cob – mealie/miele

cos lettuce – romaine lettuce

cream – if type of cream is not specified, use pouring cream, or light or single cream

eggplant – aubergine, brinjal

English spinach – baby spinach; not the heavily veined, thick-leafed vegetable sold as spinach or silver beet

fish substitutes – for blue-eye, bream, ling, snapper, flathead, use any firm, white-fleshed fish such as cod, coley, hake or kabeljou

kecap manis – sweet soy sauce

Lebanese cucumber – Mediterranean cucumber, short cucumber

oregano – oreganum

papaya – pawpaw

passionfruit – granadilla

pepitas (pumpkin seeds) – use sunflower seeds

rockmelon – cantaloupe

salt-reduced – low-sodium

silver beet – Swiss chard

Swiss brown mushrooms – brown mushrooms

telegraph cucumber – English cucumber, long cucumber

vegetable oil – use canola oil

Vietnamese mint – mint or combination of cilantro and mint

wholegrain mustard – seeded mustard

wholemeal – whole-wheat

witlof – witloof, Belgian endive

zucchini – baby marrow, courgette

WEIGHTS AND MEASURES

Ingredients are generally listed by their weight or volume with cup measurements given for convenience, unless the conversion is imperfect, whereby the ingredients are listed by weight or volume only. Sometimes conversions within a recipe are not exact but are the closest conversion that is a suitable measurement for each system. Use either the metric or the imperial measurements; do not mix the two systems.

NUTRITIONAL ANALYSIS

Each recipe is accompanied by a nutrient profile showing kilojoules (kJ), calories (kcal), protein, fat (including saturated fat), carbohydrate (including sugars), fibre and sodium. Serving suggestions, garnishes and optional ingredients are not included in the nutritional analysis. For the recipe analysis we used FoodWorks ® based on Australian and New Zealand food composition data.

OVEN TEMPERATURES

• These recipes have been written for a regular oven. If you have a fan-forced (convection) oven, reduce the temperature by 20°C.
• If you have a broiler (grill) where the temperature cannot be adjusted by a temperature dial or knob, lower the rack down from the element as follows: Medium – about half or two-thirds of the way down; Medium–hot – about a third of the way down.

CAN SIZES

Can sizes vary between countries and manufacturers; if the stated size is unavailable, use the nearest equivalent. Here are the metric and imperial measurements for can sizes used in this book:
225 g = 8 oz; 300 g = 10 oz; 350 g = 12 oz; 400/410 g = 14 oz = 398 ml/410 ml; 425 g = 15 oz = 540 ml; 800 g = 28 oz = 796 ml.

Seasonal Salads

Copy Editor Justine Harding
Designer Avril Makula
Proofreader Susan McCreery
Indexer Glenda Browne
Senior Production Controller Monique Tesoriero
Senior Designer Joanne Buckley
Editorial Project Manager Deborah Nixon

READER'S DIGEST GENERAL BOOKS

Editorial Director Lynn Lewis
Design Manager Donna Heldon

PHOTOGRAPHY CREDITS

Photographs are the copyright of Reader's Digest, except for the following, which are from Shutterstock: 6 l; 9 bl; 10 l; 10 br; 11 all; 12 l; 12 tr; 13 bl; 14 l; 14 r; 15 tl; 15 tr; 15 br; 256; and endpapers, backgrounds and decorative elements.
l = left; r = right; t= top; b = bottom

Front cover Prosciutto, pear and parmesan salad, page 192
Back cover *left* Tuna, chickpea and dill salad, page 161; *right* Pistachio and goat's cheese salad, page 83

Seasonal Salads contains some material first published in the following Reader's Digest books: *5-10-15 Cookbook (5 Ingredient Cookbook); Anti-Ageing Diet Cookbook; Complete Book of Herbs; Cooking for One or Two; Cooking series: Seasonal Cooking; Cooking series: Sensational Salads; Frische Salate und Dressings; GI Cookbook; Grandma's Quick & Thrifty Cookbook; Great Potato Cookbook; High Fibre Cookbook; Meals That Heal High Blood Pressure; Midweek Meals Made Easy; Super Foods Super Easy; Ultimate Book of Vegetables; Vegetables for Vitality*

Seasonal Salads is published by
Reader's Digest (Australia) Pty Limited,
80 Bay Street, Ultimo NSW 2007, Australia
www.readersdigest.com.au
www.readersdigest.co.nz
www.rdasia.com; www.readersdigest.ca

First published 2015
Copyright © Reader's Digest (Australia) Pty Limited 2015
Copyright © Reader's Digest Association Far East Limited 2015
Philippines Copyright © Reader's Digest Association Far East Limited 2015

National Library of Australia Cataloguing-in-Publication entry

Title: Seasonal Salads.
ISBN: 978-1-922085-87-0 (hardback)
Notes: Includes index.
Subjects: Salads
Other Creators/Contributors: Reader's Digest (Australia)
Dewey Number: 641.83

Prepress by Colourpedia, Sydney
Printed and bound by Leo Paper Products, China

We are interested in receiving your comments on the contents of this book. Write to: The Editor, General Books Editorial, Reader's Digest (Australia) Pty Limited, GPO Box 4353, Sydney, NSW 2001, or email us at bookeditors.au@readersdigest.com

To order additional copies of this book, please contact us by telephone as follows:
1300 300 030 (Australia);
0800 400 060 (New Zealand);
1800 465 0780 (Canada);
or email us at customerservice@readersdigest.com.au

Concept code: AU 0980/
Product code: 041 55